◼SCHOLASTIC

The Fluent Reader in ACTION

A **Close-Up** Look Into
15 Diverse Classrooms

Timothy V. Rasinski
Gay Fawcett
Kristin Lems
Robert Ackland

New York • Toronto • London • Auckland • Sydney
Mexico City • New Delhi • Hong Kong • Buenos Aires

Teaching *Resources*

Cover design: Emil Meek
Interior design: Holly Grundon
Cover photos: © SuperStock (middle, right)

ISBN: 978-0-439-63341-3

Copyright © 2010 by Timothy V. Rasinski, Gay Fawcett, Kristin Lems, and Robert Ackland

All rights reserved. Published by Scholastic Inc.
Printed in the U.S.A.

2 3 4 5 6 7 8 9 10   40   17 16 15 14 13 12 11

TABLE *of Contents*

Introduction

The idea of fluency first came on the contemporary literacy landscape in the late 1970s and early 1980s with the seminal work of Jay Samuels (1997) Carol Chomsky (1976), Peter Schreiber (1980), and Richard Allington (1983), among others, who argued that there is an important link between immediate word recognition and reading comprehension. It is not only important for readers to read words accurately; they also need to read the words effortlessly or automatically, so they can use the (always finite) amount of cognitive attention to attend to meaning instead of devoting it to reading the text correctly. These early fluency scholars also taught us it is important for readers to read words with appropriate expression (what linguists call "prosody") so that they are able to chunk text into meaningful phrases and add meaning through vocal emphasis, volume, speed, and pausing. Fluency, they said, was the missing link in effective literacy instruction.

Despite this early interest, reading fluency gained little attention for the next two decades. Most literacy scholars continued to focus their attention on comprehension and comprehension instruction. Many teachers asked, "Why is it important to teach children to read orally and with expression? We need to improve silent reading comprehension."

Finally, in 2000, with the publication of the report of the National Reading Panel (NICHD, 2000a, 2000b), fluency became one of the pillars of effective reading instruction. The report summarized empirical research related to fluency and its instruction, and concluded that fluency is an important part of effective reading instruction and that teaching fluency to students leads to improvement in their oral and silent comprehension and overall achievement in reading.

Since the NRP's report, research has continued to demonstrate that fluency is an important part of reading instruction at the early grade levels and beyond. Lack of fluency is often the culprit for many students who experience difficulty in reading comprehension and achievement.

Many fine books on reading fluency—such as *The Fluent Reader* by Timothy Rasinski (2010) and *What Really Matters in Fluency* by Richard Allington (2008) to name just two—have been embraced by literacy scholars, researchers, and teachers. These books provide a great introduction to fluency: defining the concept and its various components; identifying how reading fluency can be assessed and how progress in fluency can be measured; and sharing basic approaches for teaching fluency in the classroom or reading clinic.

Still, despite the growing research and scholarly writing that supports fluency, actual models of effective and engaging fluency instruction from real classrooms are scarce. Expert advice to teachers on teaching reading fluency is often misdirected—such as having children read the same passages over and over for the express purpose of increasing their reading rate. Teachers want and need models of authentic instruction in fluency from real classrooms.

Our hope is that this book will help to fill the gap in the teaching of reading fluency by providing readers with detailed models of how fluency is taught by teachers in the United States and other English-speaking countries. It offers readers the chance

* to see fluency instruction in action,

* to understand how fluency fits into the larger realm of school literacy instruction,

* to think deeply about their own approaches to instruction and assessment, and

* to make and implement their own plans for effective fluency instruction.

Defining Fluency

Just what is reading fluency? Fluency is often misunderstood as nothing more than reading quickly. But there is a much deeper view of fluency. We see fluency as the ability of readers to master the printed text—the "surface level"—so that they may reach the "deep level," gaining meaning and comprehending the text. Although achieving comprehension (deep level) is the essential goal of reading, gaining mastery of the surface level is necessary for readers to dive into meaning. Many readers fail to understand what they read, not because they can't make sense of the text (they understand just fine if the text is read to them), but because they have not yet mastered the various tasks required at the surface level. They may not be decoding the words with sufficient *accuracy* or *automaticity,* they may not be grouping the individual words in the passage into meaningful phrases, or they may not be reading the passage with meaningful expression, or prosody. Noted literacy scholars Nell Duke, Michael Pressley, and Katherine Hilden (2004) suggest that a major cause of comprehension difficulties among a significant number of students is a lack of fluency, or difficulty in dealing with the surface level of texts. So, although fluency itself may not deal exclusively with meaning, readers need to have fluency to comprehend what they read. Let's take a closer look at each of the various components of fluency.

Word Decoding Accuracy

Word decoding is what some scholars call the "phonics" component in reading. If students can decode or sound out the written words, they are accurate in their word recognition. Word decoding accuracy is the foundational component of fluency. Clearly, readers cannot read if they are unable to decode the words they encounter in print. This calls for a strong word study program in the classroom where students learn about words—how they are sounded out, how they are spelled, and what they mean. Although phonics is important, it is only part of word study. Effective word study engages students in learning about words from a variety of perspectives.

Automaticity

The theory of automaticity in reading proposed by LaBerge and Samuels (1974) suggests that all readers have a limited amount of cognitive attention. One's cognitive attention can only be divided among so many tasks. Think of your own experience trying to do two, three, or more tasks at the same time that require your attention. Chances are good that you did not do as well as you would have liked on at least one of those tasks because you were not able to give it your full attention. The high number of auto accidents by drivers using cell phones is one dramatic example of this problem.

Reading requires at least two important tasks to be done simultaneously. The first is to decode the written words. The second, more important task is to make sense of what the author is trying to convey through the written words. If readers have to give too much attention to the first task (word decoding), they may not have sufficient attention to do the second (making meaning). One of the keys to successful reading is to use a minimal amount of attention on the first task so as to have a sufficient amount for the second task. The way to minimize attention on the first task is to make it an automatic process— something that is done effortlessly. Perhaps the best example of automatic word decoding is you—the person reading this text. As an adult reader, you are likely putting very little effort into decoding the words as you read this text; you are not consciously using your phonics knowledge. Most of the words you encounter are sight words, instantly and effortlessly recognized. The result of your automaticity in word decoding is that you can give most of your attention to making meaning out of this passage.

Automaticity in word decoding needs to be part of effective reading fluency instruction. It is developed through repeated practice in identifying words, particularly repeated practice of words in written discourse or authentic reading.

Prosody

When you think of a fluent speaker, you often think of someone who speaks with good expression, using voice to make meaning in concert with the words. Fluent readers read in the same way, with expression in their voice. In doing so, they are able to demonstrate that they are making and monitoring meaning and enhancing their comprehension of their reading. Even when readers read silently, they hear their internal voice. Thus, expressive, prosodic reading applies to silent as well as oral reading. Research has found that readers who read orally with good expression are more likely to read with higher levels of comprehension when they read silently, and readers who read with lower levels of appropriate expression and prosody are more likely to read with lower levels of comprehension in their silent reading. (Daane, Campbell, Grigg, Goodman & Oranje, 2005; Pinnell et al, 1995; Rasinski, Rickli & Johnston, 2008). When teachers work with students to help them hear that "expressive voice," even when reading silently, they are asking their students to read with fluency and with good comprehension. Effective and authentic reading fluency instruction, then, needs to include a focus on having students read with appropriate expression, or prosody. Prosodic reading is best taught by modeling it, and by talking with students about how the voice is able to express meaning. Students must then have opportunities to practice prosodic reading and perhaps to perform their reading for an audience that can listen and respond.

Why This Book?

All three components of reading fluency—accuracy, automaticity, and prosody—are important and need to be part of effective reading instruction. Knowing what to teach, however, is much different than knowing *how* to teach. This book allows you to drop in on teachers who are teaching reading fluency effectively and in ways that students find engaging and enjoyable. Moreover, you will find that all the teachers we feature in this book and its companion, *The Fluent Reader in Action, Grades 5 and up*, teach the basic components of fluency, but they all teach them differently. The idea we wish to convey is that teachers make the difference. Although we know what we need to teach for fluency, how that teaching is done depends on the teacher. There is no one program or one approach that works best. There are some basic principles of teaching fluency (see the box on page 10), but how those principles are applied in real classrooms is the job of the teacher. We want you to see how different teachers, in different parts of the world, working with different children, have developed their own effective approaches to teaching fluency.

How to Use Fluency in Action

As an educator who wishes to improve literacy instruction, there are many ways that you could approach this book. You could read it all in one sitting, or over the course of days or weeks, trying new strategies and activities as you go. Perhaps the best way is to read it as part of a study group with other teachers and educators in order to create opportunities for reflection and discussion.

Before Reading

Before you read beyond this introductory chapter, think about your own approach to reading fluency. Take out a notebook that you can use to accompany your reading of this book. Then think about and respond to the following questions:

* How do you define reading fluency? What does it mean to you?

* Do you consider yourself a fluent reader? Why?

* If you are a fluent reader, how did you become one?

* Rate your own knowledge of reading fluency high, moderate, low. How did you learn about reading fluency?

* Do you feel that fluency is important enough to be taught in the reading classroom? Why?

* How much time do you allot for it on a daily or weekly basis?

* What constitutes fluency instruction in your classroom? What do you do and what do you have your students do in the name of fluency instruction?

* What sorts of texts do you use to teach and nurture fluency in your students?

* How do you connect fluency instruction with the need for students to be good at comprehending what they read? How do you help them see the connection between fluency and overall proficient reading?

* How do you assess and monitor students' progress in reading fluency?

* How do you communicate to parents and others about reading fluency?

Group Discussion

After you have responded to the questions on page 8, share your responses with others in your group. Do you have similar feelings about and experiences with fluency? Try to brainstorm as a group at least five essential questions about reading fluency that you would like to address as you engage in reading this book. Once you've done this, you are ready to dive into the chapter stories of individual teachers.

After Reading

Each chapter tells the story of a teacher who teaches at least some aspect of reading fluency in a way that is her or his own, (although all base their fluency instruction on common key fluency principles). Read the teacher's story, observe how challenges were overcome, and think about other problems that remain to be solved and next steps to be taken, especially if you are choosing to implement the model in your own classroom or instructional setting. Examine the documents and materials that are presented in each chapter.

* What's your take on these materials? Are they something you could adapt for your own teaching?

* Think about the teacher's evidence of success. Do you find it compelling? What else might need to be assessed if you were to attempt this model of instruction?

* Finally, think about how you might adapt this model (not simply transfer it) to your own instructional setting. What would you do differently to employ the model described in each chapter to fit your personal style of teaching and the kinds of students with whom you work?

Once you have thoroughly digested a chapter meet with your colleagues who are also reading this book and share the thoughts and insights that you took from each chapter. How would your colleagues approach or adapt the model of fluency instruction presented in each chapter? How do their responses change your own thinking? Go through each chapter in this way. The chapters are not long. You should be able to read and respond to each in a little more than an hour—so one or two chapters per week is a very viable approach to covering the book.

In addition to reading the chapters, you may wish to share your own approaches and successes in teaching students to read fluently. You may also wish to bring in a teacher from your school or a nearby school who is doing some interesting, innovative, and effective in fluency instruction. Videotape examples that you think are worthy of analysis and discussion. You might even want to try out some of the activities described in the book within your discussion group. Have a poetry party, engage in assessing one another's reading fluency, perform a Readers Theater script for an audience of fellow teachers or students in your school. Be sure to think about how you and your colleagues responded to these opportunities to do what you are asking your students to do.

Once you have made it through each chapter, ask yourself and your colleagues, What is going to happen as a result of my (our) reading this chapter? What will we do differently as individuals and as a group of teachers? Begin to devise a plan for making fluency instruction an important part of your school's literacy curriculum. Maybe your initial plan will consist of baby steps. That's fine. Sometimes the most effective change happens when it is done in small increments. Also, ask yourself, also, how you will assess, monitor, and report on whatever change you decide to implement. How will you be able to determine success in your fluency instruction initiative? We live in an age of increasing accountability; we need to be sure that our instructional time is spent in ways that are making a positive difference in students' lives.

We hope that after reading this book, you are as enthusiastic about reading fluency as we are. Of course, fluency is not the answer to every student's concern in reading. However, if done well, fluency instruction can make a huge difference in the lives of many children who may otherwise fall through the cracks in reading.

We thank you for giving us the opportunity to share the stories of the wonderful teachers portrayed in this book, we hope you find their stories helpful and inspiring, and we wish you all the best on your own journey toward effective reading fluency instruction.

7 Principles

for *Teaching Fluency*

1. **Word study.** Help students develop masterful accuracy in their word recognition/decoding/spelling skills, including the knowledge of the meaning of words.

2. **Modeling fluent reading.** Read to students regularly and discuss with them how you are able to make meaning with various elements of your voice while reading.

3. **Supported reading.** Provide fluent reading support (scaffolding) for students by allowing them to read along while listening to a recording of the text.

4. **Repeated reading.** Have students read particular texts several times, with the focus on reading with meaningful expression. Be sure to provide appropriate guidance and support for students while they engage in repeated readings.

5. **Phrased (syntactically appropriate) reading.** Teach students to read text in syntactically appropriate and meaningful chunks or phrases (noun, verb, prepositional phrases). Help them see that a reader's voice can help mark phrase boundaries while reading orally.

6. **Appropriate leveled texts.** Provide students with independent-level materials for reading without assistance. When students have an opportunity to practice and rehearse, you may challenge them with material that is somewhat more difficult, even occasionally at their frustration level. With supported practice, students can learn to master even challenging materials.

7. **Synergy fluency instruction.** Accomplish this by creating instructional routines that combine the principles above.

Preschool Fluency in a
Northeast Ohio Special Education Consortium

What does fluency mean in a preschool context? What does it mean for learning disabled students? Jenifer Wexler is a preschool teacher who has redefined fluency for her young learning disabled students, who, in her words, are "living language" as they struggle to understand the language around them, and begin to communicate, adding words and ideas to their repertoire. Simple stories are put into script form and students are assigned parts in order to develop language skills. The children practice their parts over and over until they meet their individualized education plan (IEP) objectives for language development. Remember: It's never too early for fluency! Oral language fluency is an important precursor to oral reading fluency.

> Fluent speakers actually help their listeners make sense of words and ideas by speaking with appropriate speed, using meaningful phrases, and embedding expression and pauses into their speech. In the same way, a fluent reader efficiently processes surface-level text information to make it as easy as possible to comprehend. (Padak & Rasinski, 2005, p. 4)

Living Language in a Preschool Classroom

Jenifer Wexler had been a teacher for 15 years—the last 8 of which were in preschool, when in 2005, she took on a very different assignment: teaching fourth-grade summer school. It was not the typical remedial summer school but rather Summer Readers' Theater, a four-week program focused on building fluency for struggling readers (see chapter 15 on Mayfield Summer Readers Theater). "I fell in love with Readers Theater," Jenifer told us. "I knew it would be a wonderful thing for my preschoolers."

In the fall, Jenifer returned to her preschool at Millridge Center for Hearing Impaired in Mayfield. At the first opportunity, she asked Tammi Bender, district literacy specialist, to help her write a $500 grant to the local Business Education Community Alliance to purchase big books, poetry, and tapes. The grant was awarded and she and her preschoolers were off and running—or perhaps we should say *off and reading*!

The Students

In her class, Jenifer usually has 12 students, ages three to six, 8 of whom are special needs children on IEPs. The identified disabilities vary each year, but it is not unusual for her to have in the same class children with Down syndrome, language delays like verbal apraxia, autism spectrum disorder, and hearing impairments.

Some of Jenifer's students don't talk at all. Some have had recent cochlear implants and are hearing for the first time and consequently just learning to talk. Other children are medically fragile, with heart problems and poor eyesight. Some are in wheelchairs. The typically-developing peers are good role models for the students with disabilities and are more tolerant and patient than most adults.

Jenifer decided to call her fluency project Living Language. She reasoned that regardless of whether they are typically-developing children or children with special needs, all of them are "living language" every day.

Preparing for Living Language

Jenifer invited Tammi to join her in bringing Living Language to her preschoolers. Together they researched what the experts in language development, early literacy, and fluency had to say. They read the works of Marie Clay (2005a, 2005b), Lea McGee and Lesley Mandel Morrow (2005), Tim Rasinski (2003), and others. Their study pointed them in the right direction as they decided what the program would look like.

They determined that the goals of Living Language would be to:

* Meet individual IEP goals

* Develop concepts of print

* Motivate learners

In addition, they identified some important procedures:

* Always hold, open, and read the book in front of children, point to words as they are read, and to talk about parts of the book.

Finally, they learned from their reading that students would be motivated by:

* a meaningful and satisfying performance using their own voices

- ✱ authentic, entertaining, and educationally powerful ways to read and communicate meaning

- ✱ growth in fluency, word recognition, and comprehension

- ✱ teacher modeling of literacy behavior

Jenifer studied each child's IEP and determined where fluency could help to meet his or her goals. She also reviewed the Ohio Preschool Standards to assure that students would be working toward skills the state expects them to achieve and that would prepare them for kindergarten. She and Tammi developed a simple rubric to aid in assessing student progress.

Living Language Lesson Plan

Jenifer's fluency program focuses on oral language fluency. She uses simple, predictable picture books that have a lot of rhyme and repetition. Each book is used for about three weeks. On the first day, Jenifer reads the book and talks with the children about the pictures and vocabulary, following the procedural guidelines mentioned earlier. Then most of the children are given a sentence strip. They practice for days until they are ready to perform their part, usually for one another, the principal, or another class.

Each child's fluency need is different, so Jenifer tailors her version of Readers Theater to the individual student. She chooses one IEP goal per child for each book. She then uses the books and poems to get them talking, following print left to right, counting words, recognizing colors, or matching syllables to her voice.

The first IEP goal for Thomas (all names are pseudonyms) was for his speech to become louder. Marie's goal was to repeat a word that had been said. Andre needed to make some sound when it was his turn. Jenifer's goal for Joseph, a typically-developing peer, was to remember and repeat his lines at the appropriate time. Marcus used his augmentative communication device during Readers Theater. His Readers Theater line was programmed into the device and the goal was for him to know when it was time for his line and to hit the correct button.

Jenifer created extension activities for each book. Some activities could require, for example, cutting pictures out of magazines or pasting pieces of a picture together.

The following are four scripts you can use for your living language lessons. For each, follow the schedule below:

Schedule:

Day 1: Read the story to the children. Then have them choral-read it back to you.

Days 2–4: Practice the story, with each child reciting his or her line.

Day 5: Perform the story for an audience.

Script #1: Autumn Sounds

Text: "Autumn Sounds" (from *25 Just-Right Plays for Emergent Readers*)

Author: Carol Pugliano-Martin

Ages: PreK–K

Instructional Group: 7 or more students

Autumn Sounds

Reader 1: Crunch! Crunch!

Reader 2: What's that sound?

Reader 3: Crunch! Crunch!

Reader 4: Look around.

Reader 5: Crunch! Crunch!

Reader 6: Hear that noise?

Reader 7: Crunch! Crunch!

Reader 8: Girls and boys?

Reader 9: Crunch! Crunch!

Reader 10: A mouse with cheese?

Reader 11: Crunch! Crunch!

Reader 12 (or All): It's autumn leaves!

Objectives

1. Students will display appropriate fluency when reading their lines.
2. Students will identify the words *crunch, leaves, mouse, cheese,* and *autumn.* (Images should accompany the words to aid identification.)
3. Students will describe what fall leaves sound like when they walk on them.
4. Students will identify how many words there are in each sentence.

Extension Activities

1. Go outside and rake up the leaves to jump in.
2. Paint precut fall leaves yellow, brown, red, and orange.
3. Sort items that are yellow, brown, red, and orange.
4. Discuss how the leaves look during the different seasons.

Script #2: The Birthday Cake

Book: *The Birthday Cake*

Author: Joy Cowley

Ages: Prek–K

Instructional Group: 7 or more students

The Birthday Cake

Narrator: "The birthday cake."

Reader 1: "A red cake."

Reader 2: "A yellow cake."

Reader 3: "A blue cake."

Reader 4: "A pink cake."

Reader 5: "A brown cake."

Reader 6: "A green cake."

All: "A birthday cake!"

Objectives

1. Students will display appropriate fluency when reading their line.
2. Students will identify colors: red, yellow, blue, pink, brown, and green.
3. Students will state the order in which the colors appear in the story.

Extension Activities

1. Cut out pictures from magazines that are the same colors as the cake. Paste them onto a premade cake made with paper of the same colors.
2. Bake a cake, using white cake mix. You can add food coloring to make the cake different colors.

Script #3: Yuck Soup

Text: *Yuck Soup*

Author: Joy Cowley

Ages: Prek–K

Instructional Group: 7 or more students (If you have more then seven students, have children read together lines together.)

Yuck Soup

Narrator: "Yuck Soup."

Reader 1: "In go some snails."

Reader 2: "In go some feathers."

Reader 3: "In go some thistles."

Reader 4: "In go some toothbrushes."

Reader 5: "In go some socks."

Reader 6: "In go some shoes."

All: "Yuck!"

Objectives

1. Students will display appropriate fluency when reading their line.
2. Students will identify the words *snails, feathers, thistles, toothbrushes, socks,* and *shoes.* (Images accompanied the words to aid identification.)
3. Students will state the order in which the food goes into the soup.
4. Students will identify how many words there are in each sentence.

Extension Activities

1. Have students make up their own "yuck soup." What would they include? Type up what they say on the computer. They could cut out pictures from magazines or draw their own to make a class book.
2. Make real soup.
3. Graph which foods the students find yucky and which foods they find yummy. Compare.
4. Have students bring in a food they think is yummy and hold taste tests.

Script #4: The Farm Concert

Text: *The Farm Concert*

Author: Joy Cowley

Ages: PreK–K

Instructional Group: 7 or more students (If you have more then seven students, have more then one child per line.)

The Farm Concert

Reader 1: "The Farm Concert"

Reader 2: "Moo, moo," went the cow.

Reader 3: "Wuff, wuff," went the dog.

Reader 4: "Quack, quack," went the duck.

Reader 5: "Croak, croak," went the frog.

Reader 6: "Oink, oink," went the pig.

Reader 7: "Baa, baa," went the sheep.

Reader 1: "Quiet!" yelled the farmer. "I can't sleep!"

Reader 2: "Moo, moo," went the cow.

Reader 3: "Wuff, wuff," went the dog.

Reader 4: "Quack, quack," went the duck.

Reader 5: "Croak, croak," went the frog.

Reader 6: "Oink, oink," went the pig.

Reader 7: "Baa, baa," went the sheep.

All: "Good," said the farmer. "I can sleep."

Objectives

1. Students will display appropriate fluency when reading their line.
2. Students will identify the noises different animals make.
3. Students will follow along with their finger as they read.
4. Students will identify how many words there are in each sentence.
5. Students will be introduced to quotation marks and exclamation points.

Extension Activities

1. Students can make puppets of one of the animals.

2. Have students choose different animal and graph their popularity.

3. Have students make a barn using milk containers, red paper, and black paper.

Evidence of Success

Jenifer videotaped the first day of Living Language. She then videotaped the final day, when the children performed. The growth for each child was dramatic. Jenifer learned that videotaping was not only a means for her to document progress, but it was also a motivational tool. She commented, "They were hams in front of the camera. They spoke louder, which, of course, was the IEP goal for some of the students."

Jenifer also kept a notebook to record progress. "When we started, they didn't know what they were doing. Each week, they got better and better. They talked a little louder, or talked more, or some were just able to finally participate." One student, whose main IEP goal was to learn to use her voice to verbalize, "really enjoys doing the little plays. She may say a couple of words. She may only give one word, but she is participating and happy about it."

Other teachers in the building observed the success of Jenifer's students and began doing Readers Theater with their students as well.

Conclusion

In the spring of her first year with Living Language, Jenifer presented the program at a meeting of the board of education. She showed the pre-program and post-program videotapes she had made, and you could have heard a pin drop. The audience was very moved by the heroic efforts and progress of her children. Board members sent Jenifer messages telling her how impressed they were with the work she and Tammi had done. One board member who is a community volunteer in Jenifer's building stopped by her room to tell her what a difference preschool teachers make.

Most teachers connect fluency instruction with traditional reading, usually oral reading. Jenifer Wexler has developed a unique program for preschoolers, many of whom have physical and mental challenges. We hope that by sharing Jenifer's story, readers have broadened their conception of fluency, reading, and especially learning.

Reflections

1. Timothy Rasinski writes in *The Fluent Reader*: "The level of vocabulary in storybooks for preschoolers is at approximately the same level as speech between college graduates." (p. 38) Do you agree? Disagree?

2. How did this chapter broaden your conception of fluency?

3. Do you have students who could benefit from oral language fluency in addition to reading fluency? What activities could you use to help them?

4. What does Jenifer's term *Living Language* mean to you?

5. Could fluency be included in IEP goals for your special education students? What goals would be appropriate for specific students?

Readers Theater Rubric

Student Name: _____ Date: _____

IEP Goal: _____

1	2	3
Rarely	Most of the Time	All of the Time

Student Handout

Readers Theater Rubric

Student Name: _____ Date: _____

IEP Goal: _____

1	2	3
Rarely	Most of the Time	All of the Time

Expressive Reading
in Newtown, New South Wales, Australia

Beginning readers often have limited sight-word vocabularies, and they benefit from opportunities to listen to and pronounce written words. Reading Recovery (Clay, 1993) and other tutoring intervention models give new readers rich opportunities to become familiar with the conventions of print. "Reading Recovery, by showing us the importance of lots of opportunity to read and reread texts that are well under control, has reminded us that daily reading of easy material is one key to fluency" (Pearson, 2004, p. 46). Repeated reading can help beginning readers who risk falling behind because the sound-print connections are hard for them (Dowhower, 1987). Turpie and Paratore (1995) found that, even at the emergent reading level, repeated reading can show measurable increases in fluency, accuracy, self-corrections, and understanding of grade-level text—all of which correlate to reading comprehension.

Repeated reading in a tutoring setting also gives learners opportunities to try out expressive, or prosodic, reading in a supportive setting. How many of us have said, "I said no and I mean no. Period!" We realize that punctuation can bring words to life. An effective tutor is able to guide young readers toward the meaning of the punctuation by modeling and scaffolding it. Zutell, Donelson, Bevans & Todt (2006) note, "Effective tutors recognize appropriate and inappropriate pitch, stress, and intonation, and provide explicit and specific models and comparisons between appropriate and inappropriate prosody. They notice and intervene when students are reading faster but not more prosodically" (p. 276). In a one-on-one tutoring session, an expert tutor can convey both expressive and "flat" reading to help a child understand that the punctuation as well as the words of the text bear meaning. Expressive reading that attends to the words and the punctuation can help unlock meaning not just for listeners but for the oral readers themselves (Dowhower, 1991). This vignette, based on two Reading Recovery lessons in an Australian primary school, illustrates just how prosody can be scaffolded in a tutoring situation, even for beginning readers.

21

Read It Like It's Talking

Stefanie McKeever is fully trained in Reading Recovery, an intervention program for struggling first-grade readers that originated in neighboring New Zealand and is widely used in Australian elementary schools. Reading Recovery includes explicit fluency instruction (Clay, 1993, 2005a). Specifically, Marie Clay states, "Fluent reading will be encouraged if the teacher:

✳ attends to the role of oral language

✳ questions so that thinking and meaning must be used

✳ increases opportunities to get fast access to the visual information in print, and arranges for plenty of practice in orchestrating complex processing on easy or instructional text levels." (Clay, 1993, p. 154)

Subsequent research on fluency has shown that struggling readers are able to handle text that is beyond their independent reading level if scaffolding is provided through support such as modeling, choral reading, and repetition (Kuhn et al., 2006; Stahl & Heubach, 2005).

Stefanie practices all of these methods in her sessions as an integral part of the Reading Recovery lesson framework.

Stefanie spends her mornings at Camdenville Public School and Preschool, in Newtown, New South Wales, as a year one (first-grade) classroom teacher; after a brief lunch, she slips into her other role as a Reading Recovery teacher, with selected children from her morning class. Camdenville, which opened in 1887 and boasts the motto "Truth and Courtesy," consists of several long buildings that form a protective square around a spacious complex with an open play area in the center. A garden plot, lovingly tended by the children, greets visitors at the entrance. The breezy classrooms of Camdenville house children from many backgrounds, including native-born Australians and immigrants, among them children whose families are economically disadvantaged. More than 10 percent of Camdenville's children come from Australia's Aboriginal population, a group that has struggled with tremendous economic, linguistic, and social challenges.

Practice in oral language is important for all readers, but even more so for English language learners like these. Once children learn the expressive, prosodic patterns of speaking in English, they will be more comfortable with the patterns when they encounter them in their reading. Choral reading, therefore, is an optimal way to promote language learning by practicing listening, speaking, and reading skills along with scaffolding (McCauley & McCauley, 1992; Stahl & Kuhn, 2002).

Reading Recovery Lessons

Stefanie's 22 students have a lively morning, studying the Maori of New Zealand and chanting out greetings in Maori; drawing and writing about a field trip they took the previous Friday to the Featherdale Wildlife Park; and working on projects in small groups. To increase exposure to rich oral language, students use headphones to listen to stories on CDs and play word-making games at the computer center. Soon, a teacher's aide comes for the children, and after putting their supplies away in their bins, it's time to march off, in jackets, sweaters, scarves, and floppy hats, to the playground and then to lunch. It has been a rich morning of conversation, listening, reading, and writing.

Now Stefanie moves into the afternoon's Reading Recovery lessons; today she has two ESL students from a small group of six in the morning class. They are in week 15 of the 20-week program, so all of the procedures have been practiced at length. Each day, Stefanie provides practice in reading fluency skills: She models expressive reading, asks questions about punctuation, reads chorally with her students, and ties questions about the story's meaning to the oral features of the characters in it.

To keep the key components of the Reading Recovery program fresh in her mind, she has 10 numbered cue cards posted on the wall above the little table at which she sits with her pupils. One highlights the need for "phrasing in fluent reading." Two other cards say "Read all the way to the full stop" and "Put them all together so that it sounds like talking." In this way, expressive reading works hand in hand with learning to read connected text.

Fluency and phonemic awareness are of special concern to the teachers in New South Wales when teaching Aboriginal children, because of the very high incidence of otitis media, a middle-ear infection that causes hearing loss. This, combined with the population's nonstandard dialect of English, makes the transition to fluent reading more challenging and the need to develop foundational oral reading skills even more important (Board of Studies, New South Wales, 2000).

Sheila, a first grader from an Aboriginal background, tugs on her braids as she sits at her small table and painstakingly reads aloud a new picture book about dogs and cats. Stefanie stops at several points to urge Sheila to predict what will happen next, and Sheila complies. Then, pointing to the varied sizes and features of the text font on the page, she asks Sheila, "When it's in black print, how does she say it?"

"She says it louder!" responds Sheila.

"She's going to chase the dog away, so how are you going to say it?" prompts Stefanie. Sheila roars, "Go away!" With satisfaction, Stefanie says, "I could hear those black words clearly!"

The next character is a cat, and Stefanie asks how it talks. "Soft voice," says Sheila, and she reads the passage, sculpting her voice accordingly. Then, says Stefanie, "See if you can make your voice go down." It seems to work. Sheila is engaged, and her expressive reading seems to aid in her ability to make predictions about the rest of the story. Further along, Sheila comes upon a yes/no question. "It's a curly one, a question mark," explains Stefanie, and models the question out loud. "Did you hear my voice go up? Can you make your voice go up, like a question?" Sheila does just that.

After focused instruction on sounds (today it's two sounds for the letter combination *oo*), putting sentences in order, rereading yesterday's book, doing a picture walk through a new one, and writing in a notebook, they wrap up the session by reading a story together chorally, a story about mushrooms. Sheila remains animated and enthusiastic throughout.

Stefanie's other student today is TJ, a Maori boy whose family has just moved to Australia from New Zealand. Stefanie gets to the topic of vocal tone right away, reading a question from yesterday's book. "Listen to my voice when I say it. What does my voice do? Can you do that?" she asks, gesturing the rising intonation with her hand. TJ has trouble reproducing it, until finally he says it like a question. "That sounds better!" says Stefanie with satisfaction. TJ rereads last Friday's book, still in a tentative style, but now with rising intonation on all of the words!

Stefanie keeps a running record as TJ reads aloud. When she notices he's over-applying the new skill, she suggests, "Can you read it like he's talking?" TJ shakes his head. She reads the text back to him, expressively, and TJ tries it again, with a considerably more varied tone. They move on to a letter sort, and he rereads a sentence he had written the previous week and plays a letter-combining game. Finally, TJ chooses a new book to read at home that night. Previewing it, Stefanie shows him how to clap out some of its two- and three-syllable words. Together, they clap syllables for "kangaroo" and "yesterday," an exercise TJ seems to relish. After receiving several stickers for meritorious reading and sharing a bit of animated conversation, TJ is walked back to class and Stefanie's instruction for the day is at an end. Tomorrow, the children will once again sample from the tasty menu of fluency activities offered by Reading Recovery.

Evidence of Success

Research on children in Reading Recovery settings has found positive program effects on standardized measures of reading achievement (D'Agostino & Murphy, 2004; Pearson, 2004). Stefanie had the following comments about the two students observed in these lessons:

> Unfortunately, Sheila is no longer at our school. My other students have, however, caught up with their peers in as little as 10 weeks, or a little over 25 hours instruction. Their confidence grows not only in reading, but in all aspects of literacy. They become much more active participants in general classroom life. In 2006, the training group of RR teachers I was involved with taught 129 students. Of these students, 87 percent were able to attain grade average. My RR training has benefited my teaching of all my regular classroom students. Without fluency, a reader soon runs out of steam. You cannot retain the meaning in complex passages if you have to laboriously decode every word."

Stefanie stresses the necessity of fluency training in literacy teaching. She says that, without it, children find comprehension difficult and the reading task daunting and irrelevant. "This year," says Stephanie, "I have really been encouraging my students, both in RR and in my guided reading sessions in my year-one class, to read the punctuation—to pay as much attention to it as to decoding the words because without it reading sounds stilted and nonsensical. To read through full-stop punctuation, for example, is to rapidly lose all meaning and vitality in a text." She continues, "Similarly, texts with plenty of dialogue give students the opportunity to get behind the characters and understand the equal importance of the narrator's voice."

Conclusion

Readers Theater is always popular . . . and adds meaning to punctuation and the need to read fluently. The writing has real purpose and the importance of fluent reading is felt and understood." Regarding the choice of texts, says Stefanie, "I think it is vital to quickly move students on from the very early 'caption' book readers, which only have one or two lines per page. I find it really important to choose stimulating texts with story lines and dialogue as soon as I feel the students can be challenged to attempt them."

"Reading is about meaning, finding out about a story, not just repeating boring exercises. Just think how many kids can confidently read dinosaur before they have mastered the difference between *get* and *got* in isolation. Reading stories encourages students to notice and attend . . . more effectively than endless drilling on flashcards and the like."

Reflections

1. What are some of the differences between practicing expressive reading in a tutoring format and in a larger class?

2. When you were a child, how often did someone read expressively to you? Have you ever read expressively to children? If so, what kinds of reactions have you observed?

3. In what ways is "fluency" a continuum, rather than a skill? Can children learn fluency even before they are literate?

4. If children come from a background in which a lot of oral storytelling occurs, how can this rich resource be used to achieve high literacy?

5. What kinds of cues could be used in a classroom to remind students of the importance of reading with expression?

6. What books do you know that are used for read-alouds that lend themselves well to prosodic or expressive reading?

Fluency Through Song
in Gwinnett County, Georgia

Repeated reading is a fluency-building strategy that consists of reading through a meaningful passage repeatedly. When reading the same passage over and over, the number of word recognition errors decreases, reading speed increases, and oral reading expression improves (Samuels, 2002).

The challenge is to find material that lends itself to repeated readings. Research has shown that the repeated reading or singing of song lyrics holds the potential for building fluency and reading comprehension (Biggs, Homan, Dedrick & Rasinski, 2008).

Fluency Through Song Lyrics

For several years, Terri Poffenberger attended reading workshops and conferences with a mission that was as much personal as professional. Of course, she wanted to learn instructional strategies to help her first-grade students in Gwinnett County, Georgia. But Terri was also hoping to find something that could help her own third-grade daughter become a fluent reader. Sammie had struggled with reading most of her school career. While she usually comprehended what she read, her laborious reading was a concern to her, her mother, and her daughter's teachers. In the summer of 2006, Terri attended a reading conference where she found what she was looking for. Terri said:

> My daughter Sammie was staying with my mother-in-law while I was at the conference. I was so excited I couldn't even wait till I got home. On the way home, I called her on my cell phone. I said to her, "I met this incredible professor. He told me how to help you go from a good reader to a phenomenal reader!" She couldn't wait for me to get home.

At the conference, Terri heard Timothy Rasinski talk about using song lyrics to promote fluency. The strategy is easy. Provide students with lyrics for their favorite songs and have them read the lyrics over and over and over. Sammie loved music and had four or five favorite CDs of Disney songs. Terri wanted to get started right away, and typed up the lyrics to three CDs. Sammie was delighted. For the next week, she spent hours reading the lyrics as she played the music. Sammie says: "There were a lot of big words. I tried sounding them out, and I couldn't get it to work. Then I tried chunking and that helped a little. Then I practiced with the music, and finally, one day I got it."

It wasn't long before Sammie was ready for more lyrics to read. Terri went on the Internet and found lyrics to more children's music that Sammie loved. Sammie created a notebook and "literally spent hours with those CDs. She would put the CD on and take out the lyrics and read along," says Terri. And as she did, Terri began to see the reading progress she had been hoping for.

"Sammie's fluency has improved more than I could ever have imagined," comments Terri. In addition, her confidence has soared—no small matter. There was a time when she would never have attempted a long or difficult book. Now her favorites are Junie B. Jones and Hannah Montana chapter books. This little girl who struggled for so long now says, "When you read a chapter book, and you read just one chapter, you want to know more about the adventures the characters are having." Sammie's teacher is pleased, and even a bit surprised, with the progress she has observed in a very short time.

Months after Terri presented her daughter with the gift of fluency at Grandma's house, Sammie continues to love her lyrics notebook and Terri is continually adding lyrics from more songs. Sammie keeps a headset in the car all the time so that she can grab her notebook on the way out the door and practice when traveling.

Sammie says, "My song notebook has helped me two ways. It helps me with reading and with learning the words to my songs. I really like it a lot." She describes herself as a good reader and says she likes to read chapter books, picture books, and about 100 songs. "Sometimes I read to my brother. He's six."

Song Lyrics Lesson Plan

Early on, Terri was so encouraged by Sammie's progress that she decided to use the strategy with her first graders. She filled numerous folders with CDs and song lyrics and placed them in the class literacy centers. There are a variety of choices. Terri says, "I find that whatever the kids are listening to and is appropriate for elementary school is what you want—*High School Musical*, Dr. Jean, and so on. Plus, I provide some CDs that have learning attached to them, like color words or numbers." Students gather a folder, a headset, and a CD, and go to work with fluency during literacy center time. The rule is that students have to read along with the music. Terri reports that they "simply love it."

Of course, it can get rowdy. You have to train the children about how loud they can be when they have a headset on, but after that, it works out well.

Besides, it's hilarious to hear a child so engaged that they are belting out a song during your reading group. You know that child is so into what he's doing he doesn't realize there's a world around him.

Terri and her class sing a song or recite a poem as a whole group every week. They usually sing during their comprehension work time in the morning. Terri puts the song lyrics on charts to introduce them and students are each given a copy of the lyrics. Sometimes, Terri puts song lyrics on the overhead projector, but it's not her favorite way to conduct the fluency practice. "There's something about having the children gathered around at our group area that just has a warm feeling that I like, says Terri. "I remember singing with my mom at the piano. Who knows? Maybe that's where I learned to read, too, and it was such a great feeling. I want the children to feel that way about our reading time together."

Terri's fluency instruction is not limited to song lyrics. Her students have poetry notebooks, and there are poems posted on chart paper around the room. Some of the poems in the poetry notebook are written by the children. Her students also learn nursery rhymes.

During literacy centers, students are encouraged to go to "browsing boxes," where they find leveled books they have been reading all year. The poetry notebooks are also kept in a browsing box. The students get to choose which books out of the browsing boxes they read, and the poetry notebooks are a definite favorite. Terri shares, "You can hear kids singing and reciting poetry all over the room. I've caught myself several times starting to remind them about the noise level and then realizing that they were working on their poetry notebooks." On weekends they take their poetry notebooks home for practice.

The poetry notebooks also contain song lyrics. Terri uses old favorites like "Itsy Bitsy Spider." Terri puts the words on chart paper and then the children do a copy change. For example, "Itsy Bitsy Spider" might become "Big, Gigantic Spider" or "Fuzzy Wuzzy Chicken." She puts the new words on sticky notes and the children use the charts during literacy centers. Terri also uses seasonal songs:

I get my song ideas from other teachers, the radio, and searching the Internet for children's songs. I have a guitar that I use with the songs from time to time. Usually it just takes a quick Internet search to find the guitar chords for the songs. My kids love it, and the teacher next door and her class join us occasionally. For my struggling readers, it gives them confidence. For the ones who are already confident readers, it is exposing them to vocabulary and concepts that we wouldn't be able to discuss just using our reading curriculum. I have had many parents comment on how they didn't think their child would be able to read the songs in the poetry notebook. They tell me how shocked and proud they were when they were able to read them.

Evidence of Success

Terri's school is in rural Gwinnett County, Georgia, where the poverty rate is high. The ESOL (The population of English language learners (ELLs) population is increasing. Many students begin school with language deficits, so it is not surprising that test scores are typically low. Terri believes her strategy is especially good for the ELL students. They are learning language and fluency at the same time. She describes her current class as "really hard—young and low level." She then pauses and corrects herself: "Well, at least they started low, but now there are only four kids below level." Terri has recorded measurable differences in fluency as she does running records, and she credits much of the gain to having songs and lyrics. "They are a very musical group."

Terri shared the strategy with the first-grade team and the special education teacher. The special education teacher found it especially effective with an autistic child. Now word has gotten around, and the kindergarten teachers and the ESOL teacher have also started using song lyrics.

Conclusion

"All those old songs. All the music. I love to sing with kids. Why did we stop singing to children?" asks Terri. Maybe more teachers like Terri will start singing with children, and in the process create more fluent readers like Sammie, who now says, "I really, really, really like reading! It's fun!"

Where to Find Songs for the Classroom

judyanddavid.com
At the Children's Music Archive, you will find lyrics, sing-along suggestions, coloring sheets, and activities.

bussongs.com
The Bus Songs website has lyrics, videos, and music for 2,072 kid's songs and nursery rhymes.

theteachersguide.com/ childrenssongs.htm
You will find recordings of hundreds of children's songs along with printable lyrics on Teacher Created Resources.

niehs.nih.gov
The National Institute of Environmental Health's Kids' Pages offers lyrics for dozens of children's songs, patriotic songs, holiday songs, and songs from movies.

kididdles.com
KiDiddles offers words to 2,000 of the most popular children's songs organized both alphabetically and by subject.

songsforteaching.com
At the Songs for Teaching website, you will find songs to support each of your curricular areas—listed by subject.

Reflections

1. Do you think your students attend to meaning when they are reading orally, or are they focused on not making errors? Provide evidence for your answer.

2. How can you help students feel comfortable enough with reading aloud that they are hearing the meaning behind their words?

3. How important is it to know the readability level before a student is assigned to read a text?

4. Do you enjoy singing? Do your students enjoy singing? Students can easily memorize songs and other rhythmical texts and may not look as closely as they should at the text as they sing. Think of ways to keep students' eyes focused on the text as they sing.

5. List all the songs you hear during a day—commercials, jump-rope jingles, radio tunes, songs from music class, theme songs for television shows, and others. Which songs would your students enjoy reading and singing?

6. How can you make sure that students are actually reading the lyrics and not just singing from memory?

Getting Parents Involved

in Mayfield Heights, Ohio

"Children who have parents who participate in their schooling have better attendance, have more positive relationships towards school, and achieve at higher levels" (National PTA, 1997, p. 19). For decades, the research has consistently indicated that student achievement increases as parents become more involved in their children's education (Berliner & Casanova, 1997; Epstein, 1984; Henderson, 1988; Postlewaite & Ross, 1992; Williams & Chavkin, 1989). But teachers and administrators don't need researchers or the National PTA to tell them this. They see it every day.

The good news is that for the most part, parents are eager to help their children with reading. The age-old advice given to parents is "Read to your child," and that's good advice indeed! However, many parents, especially those of struggling readers, want to do more than read aloud and practice flashcards.

Reading fluency is not a difficult concept for parents to understand, and it's not a difficult one for them to work on at home. One way to encourage parents to help their children develop fluency is to regularly send home copies of nursery rhymes or poems for practice, sometimes accompanied by short activities that help children practice other reading skills.

A Structure for Parent Involvement

The four first-grade teachers at Mayfield, Ohio's Lander Elementary School were keenly aware of six-year-olds' need for structure. Each year, they spent plenty of time up front teaching their new students the daily schedule, classroom routines, and behavior expectations. Their balanced literacy program was also structured with a set time for reading, writing, and oral language; a combination of whole group, small group, and individual instruction; and just the right amount of explicit teacher instruction and independent student work. Things ran smoothly for the well-planned program, except for one thing—parent involvement.

A Close-Up Look Into **15 Diverse Classrooms**

31

For years, the first-grade team had requested that their students practice reading at home with parent support. Students were required to keep a nightly reading log, and parents were asked to sign the log. "It was pretty random," teacher Barb Tarka admits. A few students read quality books every night. For most students, however, the time they spent reading and the quality of books they read were hit-and-miss. What haunted the teachers most were those students who owned few books and did not have a library card. "These were the kids who needed extra reading time most, and the homework was just one more thing that prevented it from happening," Barb shares.

The Fast-Start Program

One day, Barb was looking through her Scholastic Book Club monthly order form and saw a teacher resource for grades K–2 titled *Fast Start for Early Readers: A Research-Based, Send-Home Literacy Program With 60 Reproducible Poems and Activities That Ensures Reading Success for Every Child* (Padak & Rasinski, 2005). "This sounded like an approach that would be much more focused than what we were doing. It hit me! Maybe our parents need structure, too!" Barb says, laughing. "I ordered it with my bonus points."

When the book arrived, Barb liked what she saw. The program is structured so that children take home one or two poems a week, including classic nursery rhymes, simple and engaging poems, and poems that can be sung to familiar tunes. "You can never have too much poetry!" Barb proclaims. Families spend 10 minutes per night with the Fast Start routine: (1) Read to your child; (2) Read with your child (choral reading); (3) Listen to your child read to you. Family Pages are also part of the nightly routine—the pages direct them to play with words from the poems: locate rhyming words; "stretch" out a word; play Word Concentration, Go Fish, or Word Bingo; listen for long or short vowels; find compound words, and so on.

Barb shared the program with the other first-grade teachers, Concetta DiGeronimo, Carol Ianiro, and Mary Hartnett. The team agreed this program sounded like it would add the needed structure for parent involvement in children's literacy development.

Implementation Plan

"When we introduce it at the beginning, we demonstrate in the classroom exactly what we expect children and parents to do at home," Barb explains. The teachers put poems on a transparency, and every morning for the first week, the classes read the poems over and over, with the teachers modeling and explicitly discussing fluency. After the first week, parents receive a letter explaining the program, and then it belongs to them and their children.

On Mondays, each student takes home a poem or rhyme copied from Fast Start, along with the activities designed for the poem. This becomes their Monday through Thursday reading homework. At the beginning of the year, it takes students about 20 minutes to complete. As the year progresses, the time commitment is 10 to 15 minutes per evening.

The teachers tell parents that if it takes longer than that, they want to know. Above all, they want the nightly reading to be pleasurable for parent and child.

Each child has a three-ring binder poetry notebook where weekly poems are saved. In addition, the notebooks have sections for word sorts, jokes and riddles, vocabulary, and other miscellaneous reading activities. As a class, the students frequently take out their notebooks and reread the poems. Barb observes, "Often, when they have free time, they go back and reread their favorites."

The teachers modified the reading log that comes with the program to better meet their specific needs. Parents use the log to check off activities their children complete. The activities might include working with words and letters, playing with sounds, or beginning to read. The form also includes a space for parents and students to list any other reading they have done. At the beginning of the year, the teachers check the reading log daily, not to assign a grade but rather to get information about which students might need additional teacher attention. As the year progresses, they check logs weekly.

Besides creating the customized reading log, the first-grade teachers have done a number of other things to make the program work well in their setting. For example, they have sequenced the poems and nursery rhymes to match the seasons and to get progressively more difficult as the year goes on.

The teachers also brought in the building's teacher of gifted and talented, Rae Malenda. Rae provided a resource book to be used with accelerated readers, *A.C.T. 1: Affective Cognitive Thinking: Thinking Strategies for the Gifted* (Blymire, Brunner, Jones & Knauer, 1982). The teachers use most of the same poems and nursery rhymes with the accelerated readers, but take activities from Rae's book that are more developmentally appropriate.

Beginning of the Year Parent Letter

Dear Families,

Learning to read is an important goal for your child this year. While we will be working on this goal every day in our classroom, you also have an essential part to play at home! This year we will participate in the Fast Start program. Fast Start is a set of short poems and wordplay activities for you and your child to do together. Please spend 10 to 15 minutes each evening on Fast Start activities with your child. Here is how the program works.

Each Monday, I will send a new poem and its family activity page in a separate Reading Log folder. Blank Reading Log sheets will be in the middle prong section.

The **Fast Start** routine is simple: Enjoy the poem together each evening.

Then . . .
Spend 10–15 minutes each evening doing the activities on the family page. Please try to do at least one activity from each of the three sections during the week. Record each evening's activity on the Reading Log sheet. We will check the logs periodically throughout the week. The Reading Log folder must be returned to school each day.

During the week, please also record other books you have read with your child. If a school week has less than 5 days, please try to complete at least 4 days of reading activities. It is through constant practice that your child will prove his or her reading skills and make progress as a reader.

Enjoy this time with your child!

First-Grade Reading Log

Student Name: _____ Date: _____

Text: _____

Day	Activities Chosen	Other Books/Poems Read
Monday _____	• Looking at Words and Letters • Playing with Sounds • Beginning to Read	
Tuesday _____	• Looking at Words and Letters • Playing with Sounds • Beginning to Read	
Wednesday _____	• Looking at Words and Letters • Playing with Sounds • Beginning to Read	
Thursday _____	• Looking at Words and Letters • Playing with Sounds • Beginning to Read	

10/05

Comments: _____
_____
_____

When the beginning readers are working on rhyming sounds, the accelerated readers may be brainstorming what they could do with a broken Humpty Dumpty, speculating why Mother Hubbard's cupboard was bare, or discussing problems a cow might have in outer space. '

The regular first-grade reading program at Lander Elementary is based on the five components of reading as identified by the National Reading Panel (2000): phonemic awareness, phonics, comprehension, vocabulary, and fluency. Every day, instruction deals with one of the components, not to the exclusion of the others, but to assure balance through focused instruction. "Fluency Friday," for instance, always includes poems from past Fast Start work. Students do choral reading or Readers Theater for their own class or for other classes. Barb says, "The students really love it—especially Fluency Friday. It's exciting to see children so enthused about reading. It's very powerful."

Evidence of Success

To measure the effectiveness of parental involvement through Fast Start, Barb gave her students the 3-Minute Reading Assessment (Rasinski & Padak, 2004) in January and again in May. In just four months, 17 of 19 students showed growth in word accuracy/decoding, with improvement as high as 25 percent. Eight students improved 10 percent or more. All but two students showed positive gains in fluency (expression and volume, phrasing, smoothness, and pace) as measured by a multidimensional fluency scale.

The four teachers also sent home a parent survey about Fast Start. Forty-three surveys were returned, a strong return rate of over 50 percent. The majority of parents reported that their children enjoy the nightly routine. About three of every four parents indicated that some of the poems were new and some were familiar to their child. Twenty-one percent said the poems were new to their child, a fact that might be explained in part by the high population of English language learners in the district. Most parents felt the activities matched their child's reading growth. Parent comments included:

> "I like this program. My older two boys did not have this. I like the structure and simplicity."

> "We have fun singing the poems out loud."

> "He slowly reads more and more with less of my help."

> "Some [of the poems] were challenging at first, but by end of the week, they became easier."

Conclusion

Fluency has been and to some extent continues to be a neglected goal of the school reading curriculum (Allington, 1983; Rasinski & Zutell, 1996). Much emphasis is placed on comprehension, and that is good. However, unless students have some degree of reading fluency, comprehension strategy instruction may not have the desired impact on student reading performance and achievement (Willingham, 2006). Most parents are eager to help their young readers. Whether you use a commercial program such as Fast Start or design fluency homework of your own, the potential payoff is great.

Reflections

1. How do you explain the concept of fluency to your beginning readers and their parents?

2. What poems do you currently use in class that could be targeted for nightly fluency practice?

3. Role-play a conversation with a parent in which you explain your fluency homework program.

4. List some of the literacy and non-literacy benefits of learning nursery rhymes.

5. Many teachers claim that today's children do not learn nursery rhymes as children once did. Do you agree? If so, how do you explain that change?

6. How would you deal with a situation where the parent does not help his or her child with the nightly fluency practice, thus putting the child at a disadvantage?

Reading and Relaxing
in Naperville, Illinois

Fluency is not only about reading aloud. It's also about gaining a comfort zone by practicing extensive silent reading (Rasinski & Hoffman, 2003). In a balanced literacy classroom that includes fluency instruction, there are many opportunities to read within the school day (Fisher & Berliner, 1985), both oral and silent. When Steven Stahl conducted a study to see the relative benefits of monitored, wide silent reading or repeated oral reading with feedback, he found that both of these techniques improved student reading comprehension more than instruction with a basal. The common element was "the increased amount of reading and the support given during the reading" (2004, p. 205). The careful support provided during reading gives children both the language to talk about their fluency and the practice needed to learn to self-monitor their oral and silent reading. D. Ray Reutzel calls this kind of work a chance for students to develop "a propensity to monitor the status of their own reading fluency" (Reutzel, 2006, p. 70). This chapter features an innovative program that comfortably combines oral reading and silent reading with strong support while children learn to self-monitor and choose appropriate-level books.

The Read and Relax Program

Although much of the general public still holds to the myth that teaching is an easy job (after all, "teachers get summers off!"), anyone who is a teacher or lives with a teacher knows about the Sunday lesson planning, the late-night paper grading, and the summers spent in graduate school. But by far the most difficult part of teaching is developing quality programs that will engage an increasingly diverse population of students. Teaching is joyful, but it is hard work. So it certainly is refreshing when a teacher describes a successful reading program as "the easiest thing I do as a teacher."

Noreen Maro has taught second grade at River Woods Elementary School in Naperville, Illinois for 15 years. Naperville is an affluent Chicago suburb that enjoys a strong

reputation among teachers. "People don't leave Naperville. They either retire or their spouses are transferred," says Noreen. She notes that 800 applications were received for two teaching positions the previous year. The positive atmosphere is palpable. "Teachers aren't competitive. They share everything they have," she says.

Noreen's "easiest thing" is a fluency-based program called Read and Relax (R&R), which she created for her second-grade classroom. She understands that one important way to increase fluency is to provide lots of opportunities for students to read successfully at an independent level. She piloted the program in her own class for several years, and eventually word got around. Soon it was adopted in grades one through five at her school. When both morale and scores at River Woods soared, the entire district adopted Read and Relax (Maro, 2001).

Read and Relax Lesson Plan

The core of Read and Relax is independent reading for 30 to 40 minutes per day. "We never miss a day of R&R!" Noreen states. Students choose their own books from a classroom library and can read anything in the room that is at their level. At the end of the allotted time, students get into groups of two or three and talk for 10 minutes about what they have read and what they want to read next.

R&R is different from Sustained Silent Reading (SSR) or Drop Everything and Read (DEAR), because the focus is on fluency. On a regular basis, just before students go off to read independently, Noreen conducts mini-lessons. She may model the rate and expression of a fluent reader or ask a fluent reader to demonstrate. She also might talk about automaticity or prosody in kid-friendly terms. The students discuss what they have heard and are encouraged to apply it as they read. Noreen also models how to choose appropriate books, circulates to make sure all students are reading texts appropriate to their level, and works one-on-one with fluency strategies for striving readers.

The element of choosing appropriate texts is the place where teacher judgment comes into play, says Noreen. "I get to know the children and I get to know the books. I look at the children and I look at the books and I know when it's a match. If the book is too difficult, the student cannot read fluently." To offer good choices, of course, it is necessary to have a rich classroom library. Noreen's classroom library consists of about 3,000 books! She is continually enhancing the library and pays close attention to its upkeep. For example, she recently made it a goal to include more informational text in her collection. "I used to have two totes of nonfiction. Now I have eight," she remarks.

Noreen says that she does a lot of steering at the beginning of the year, but as the program evolves, students come to know what they can handle. "It's to a point that if I walk up behind them, they start to read aloud, and when I fade away they go back to reading silently. If I note problems with fluency, I sit down and work with the child." Noreen believes it is important to be comfortable and supportive with reading struggles. "I let them know that it's acceptable. Mistakes are expected, inspected, and respected," she states. "That's the only way they're going to learn."

R&R in a Balanced Literacy Program

In addition to silent reading, Noreen's students do other fluency building activities, including performing poetry, Readers Theater, and plays from reading *Safari Magazine*, which has a play in each issue. "I make sure lower-level students read a play, I invite in a few higher-level readers, and they all perform it."

Noreen's students also do quite a bit of writing, including "life books" and chapter books. The more they read, the more genres they are willing to try to write. Noreen can see that the books children are reading in R&R and the writing of their own classmates influence their writing. Much to Noreen's delight, students have even asked, "Can we make connections with other students' writing?"

Noreen's students write a tremendous amount of poetry. Each year, the class publishes a poetry anthology of original student work. Some other classes are now doing it, and her teaching partner won a grant from a grocery store chain to publish student writing online. The teaching partner typed all of the poems, which took "days and days," and after the collection was published online, she produced copies of the writing to give to the students.

How Read and Relax Has Evolved

R&R has now been in use for several years in all of the K–5 schools in Noreen's district. As it is implemented in more diverse settings, it is also being adapted. Noreen has made structural modifications of her own. She used to require that books stay in the classroom, but now she lets students take chapter books home so they can finish them. Another of Noreen's adaptations is paired feedback at the end of the silent reading. "One of the students said to me, 'What I was reading wasn't clear until I tried to describe it to somebody else.' Sometimes I ask students to read orally to one another, thus giving them one more opportunity to demonstrate fluency."

In reflecting on how R&R works with English language learners (ELLs) in guided reading groups, Noreen has discovered that there may be ELLs who are "reading and doing all right, a little quiet, so you don't really get to know them. Then during Read and Relax, the same child grabs a book that during guided reading I would have thought was too difficult for them, and I move them up a group!" She discovered that, due to shyness and the silent period many ELLs experience, they tend to read at a higher level in independent reading than they do when reading aloud from basals for guided reading (Gass & Selinker; Lems, Miller & Soro, 2010).

Building an R&R Program

River Woods Elementary has the fewest low-income students of the 21 schools in District 203 with only 4.5 percent. Therefore, there are factors operating in its favor—low student mobility, teacher stability, and a strong funding base—that may be hard to replicate in less affluent districts. Nonetheless, R&R can be implemented anywhere if the necessary pieces are in place.

One of those pieces is having a good library in every classroom. Noreen observes that teachers hired right out of college tend to come without books, and they need to learn to build classroom libraries. Although this is easier in more affluent districts, it is possible to build a good classroom library in any district. For example, Kingsley Elementary, another school in District 203, partnered with its parent organization in a fundraiser to buy books for classroom libraries. At River Woods, a teacher wrote a grant and received 20 to 30 boxes of books at the kindergarten through second-grade level. Because of this grant, students were able to check out books and keep them for two weeks, then get new books; parent volunteers handled the checkout and tallied the books. Finally, Scholastic Book Club gives many grants and incentives connected with book fairs. "If there's a will, there's a way!" declares Noreen.

Evidence of Success

River Woods Elementary, along with the other schools in District 203, collects fluency data, and these support the claim that R&R is a positive presence in the school. The school administers one-minute oral reading tests at the beginning, middle, and end of the year.

Although the district-wide rate study wasn't designed to assess the R&R program per se, its scores reflect the improvement that comes about when children do a large amount of independent reading. The recent school-wide reading rate study showed significant improvement as well. "Some second graders who read 12 words per minute at the beginning of the school year, for example, were reading 100 words per minute by January," Noreen reports proudly.

When R&R was implemented in schools elsewhere in Naperville, including a school with a larger number of at-risk students, the improvement in reading rate after four months was what the teachers called "phenomenal." River Woods was awarded the Academic Excellence Award of the Illinois State Board of Education, because 90 percent or more of its students in grades three through five read at or above grade level, and the whole school successfully met NCLB targets. Beyond the impressive test scores, there are other, more dramatic advantages. "Children develop a love of reading," says Noreen. "I've had boys who didn't want to go to gym, because they were enjoying a book so much."

Noreen checked up on some of her former students to see if they had continued any of the practices they experienced with R&R. Here is what she found:

> I called kids I had taught who were now in junior high. They had been my students the second year I taught. One of the girls had started a reading club. They'd get together and read. I called another who had started reading at 20 words per minute and gotten up to 220. She immediately started talking about the series she was into.

Another positive effect can be seen in the sense of community a class builds up over the year. Students like to share with classmates what they read and write, and this helps children become more trusting of others. "I decided with my teaching partner to build a sense of community in the classroom. What we found out at the end of the year is that there weren't behavioral problems, and we had come together as a community." She attributes this mainly to the positive environment created by the reading and sharing of R&R.

Conclusion

Beyond the funding, planning a good classroom library for an independent reading program such as R&R requires thought and reflection on the part of the teacher and the school literacy leadership. Books in several genres and at many reading levels are needed. There should be a good checkout and cataloging system so that the collection is maintained. Asking for help from a school librarian or a veteran teacher is highly recommended. Also, books need to be replaced when they become tattered or lost. Teachers can refresh their collections at the end of each year or during the winter holiday break so they are in good working order at the start of classes.

Another important consideration in having an R&R program is administrative and teacher buy-in. Success depends upon "how religiously you do it. If teachers don't monitor, and students are choosing books that are too difficult, the program actually inhibits their growth and has an adverse effect," Noreen cautions. The school literacy team needs to provide regular opportunities for dialogue, professional development, and informal observations so that the program is implemented conscientiously and faithfully. The team also needs to get regular feedback from other teachers who are implementing R&R.

Noreen Maro is thrilled to see R&R used for a larger group of students and to have it included in this book. "I love to share it. It's so good for kids! Clearly, many of us in our busy lives could use a little R&R!" Find a good book and try a little Read and Relax yourself. It could be the easiest thing you do!

Reflections

1. If you are in a teaching setting, what elements of Noreen's balanced literacy program are already in place there? Which ones could be tried out?

2. What are some of the advantages of having a classroom library in addition to a school library?

3. What are some ways to steer a child toward a book that is at his or her independent reading level? Could it ever be useful to make exceptions to this? If so, when?

4. What are some of the places where teachers can obtain low-cost or free children's books in your community? From outside sources?

5. When adults do sustained silent reading, they often have a favorite spot or time of day to do it. Some want to sit in a comfortable chair with a warm cup of coffee. Others like reading on the train. Share some examples of adult reading habits you have practiced or observed.

Teacher Action Research

in Salisbury, Maryland

Every few years, a word or phrase grabs the spotlight in education. We read about it, write about it, try to implement it, and often we then move on to a new "hot topic." *Scientifically based reading research* seems to be the phrase that currently sell publishers' wares or assures program approval by No Child Left Behind legislators. The term appears in the NCLB law 111 times, perhaps justifiably so; it is essential that reading instruction be supported by research that meets rigorous standards.

Scientifically-based-reading research can inform teachers, but as Catherine Compton-Lilly observes in *Promoting Teachers at Researchers,* "Teachers are the ones who have real connections with children and families. The stories we can tell about actual classroom practices, as well as about families' and communities' responses to those practices, are extremely valuable" (International Reading Association, 2004, p. 7).

Teachers who do "action research" raise questions about what is happening in their classrooms. They observe, examine student work, study test data, try new things, and analyze what they find to improve teaching and learning. Teacher research into students' reading fluency or teachers' fluency instruction can be a powerful catalyst for improving reading achievement.

Fluency Through Wide Reading

A teacher in Salisbury, Maryland, Michelle White reads every issue of *The Reading Teacher* from cover to cover and always finds something she can use to improve her teaching and her students' learning. When she picked up the October 2004 issue, however, she found something that would transform her and her students. Michelle was to become a dedicated teacher researcher while her students would become fluent readers. Michelle talks about how it all began:

> I read Lorraine Wiebe Griffith and Timothy Rasinski's article "A Focus on Fluency: How One Teacher Incorporated Fluency With Her Reading

Curriculum" (2004). Her results from year one showed the class averaged 2.5 years' growth in reading comprehension and fluency. I wanted this for my students! This would be worthwhile research to duplicate. I began implementing her three-year plan.

The Implementation Plan

One: Readers Theater

Following Griffith's outline, Michelle began the first year of her action research with a focus on Readers Theater. That year, she was assigned to teach mostly above-level second-grade readers. Although most teachers recognize the need for fluency instruction with struggling readers, Michelle was excited to try it with her capable readers. She explains:

> I figured if Readers Theater could help struggling readers improve their reading, then it could help above-level readers become even stronger fluent readers. However, there were also a few students in the group who were not high-level readers. Their reading was very choppy. They read without expression and at different rates. One minute they read fast, and the next minute they read slowly. Their word automaticity was weak. Sometimes they needed to sound out words. I could tell they did not comprehend, because sentences that were to be funny or were to express some kind of feeling were read with no expression. I knew this plan was especially going to help them.

Michelle used stories from the district-adopted Houghton Mifflin reading series *The Nation's Choice* (2003) for Readers Theater. She found scripting tips from Aaron Shepard's website (aaronshep.com) very helpful in turning the stories into scripts. She explains how it worked: "On Mondays, I simply assigned students a page at random from their anthology or a Readers Theater script. On average, each student had about 30 words to practice nightly for homework. On Fridays, the class would take 10 to 15 minutes to read the script or story aloud."

Michelle sent a letter to parents explaining the importance of fluency, what Readers Theater is, and their role in supervising the homework practice. On Fridays, the second graders performed for their parents, who crowded into the classroom to watch. In a short time, Readers Theater began to take on a life of its own, one Michelle and her students created. She explains it this way:

> They would start about Wednesday asking, 'Is it Friday? Are we going to do it? Are we going to do it?' They loved pretending they were the characters. Although we started with the Readers Theater model of no

costumes, they would dress up anyway because they were so excited.
One story had a cowboy theme and two or three came in cowboy getups.
Finally I started joining them. I would step out of the room for a second
and I would get dressed up for the performance."

Year Two: Automaticity

Michelle was gratified with the progress her advanced students made in year one, so there was no question that she would continue action research in year two. Now, however, she wanted to gather data that would support the usefulness of fluency activities with struggling readers as well as typically-developing readers. Michelle implemented the fluency plan with her heterogeneous second-grade homeroom during her language arts block. At the same time, she implemented the program with the group of struggling readers she was assigned to teach that year.

Michelle's overall goal during the second year was for the students to increase their reading word recognition automaticity (measured by reading rate), which she believed would improve reading comprehension. Michelle followed Griffith's year two action research plan by adding timed reads and partner reads, while continuing the Readers Theater routine.

For the timed reads, students were given passages at their individual reading levels that were taken from the Houghton Mifflin series or from library books they chose. Michelle chose additional selections from children's magazines that supported their science and social studies curricula. They read aloud their 120-word passage to a partner using expression and a normal rate. After 60 seconds, they marked where they ended reading and recorded the number of words read. They repeated this process in order to track their progress after each timed read.

During sustained silent reading, each student paired with a partner who shared similar reading interests. The partners read together silently for about 10 minutes, then took turns reading aloud. Michelle gathered data on their progress during this time by walking around the room and listening to the pairs read. Right away, she noticed that students had more confidence and were reading at a smoother pace.

Since the students were using authentic literature in their paired and timed reads, Michelle seized the opportunity to discuss elements of good writing, another component of Griffith's action research.

There were several special needs students in the heterogeneous group. Two in particular were very low readers. Aaron* was officially coded as a "non-reader." The other student, Michael, read at a kindergarten level. Michelle describes how these students responded to the fluency instruction:

Readers Theater gave them the opportunity to read successfully. I didn't
give them as many lines. It really made them feel part of the class. Before
this, Aaron, the non-reader, wasn't really part of the reading class. Now, on

All names are pseudonyms.

Friday, he could read his line. He would look at the paper and point to the words. Every time he read, he would look up with the biggest smile on his face. It looked like he was thinking, I did it! I did it! Just to see their little faces…And then there was Michael, who was at the 24th percentile on the Stanford 10 at the end of first grade. By the end of second grade, Michael's reading score had improved to the 65th percentile.

Readers Theater, timed reading, and partner reading helped some children move to an on-level reading group. One day, Zach said to Michelle, "You told me if I practiced, I would be able to read. You were right!"

Frequently, Michelle's group of struggling readers performed their Readers Theater for the kindergarten class on Fridays. The kindergarten teacher Antoinette Perry (who is now a vice-principal) reflects on the experience:

> The younger students get a chance to have other children read to them.
> Many times, they hear adults reading to them and feel that reading is for
> the adults only. When the older students came to read to them, I explained
> that they would be reading like that soon. This made my students want to
> learn to read. Each Friday, they questioned whether or not their "special
> readers" were coming to the class.

Michelle's students didn't want to miss school on Fridays. Often, when they had stayed home sick, parents would bring them to school just in time for the performance. One parent commented, "You took a little boy who loves to read and truly began to instill a love of learning that will last a lifetime."

Year Three: The Rollout

In year three, Michelle accepted a position as reading coach for the district, serving two elementary buildings. The research continued, albeit in a different way. Her goal for year three was to help other teachers understand the power of what she had been doing with fluency instruction. She modeled lessons in classrooms and held workshops at the county level. After attending one of Michelle's workshops, Charmaine, a fourth-grade teacher, wrote to her:

> I tried Readers Theater with my kids today, and they responded well. I had
> them count off 1 to 4 and then I broke them into groups. Each number
> corresponded to a part in the script, which they read and reread. Then
> I randomly called out a number and let the children with that number
> switch groups. That kept it interesting, and they didn't even realize they
> had read the passage about 10 times by the time we were done. I also
> encouraged them to read with accents or silly voices—as long as they were
> reading the right words. It was really successful.

Evidence of Success

To gauge the success of the fluency action research project, Michelle administered leveled reading passages from the Houghton Mifflin series. This assessment measured students' reading levels and included fluency, comprehension, and retelling. The assessment was administered in October, February, and May to establish a baseline and to show growth.

In year one, the classroom grade-level average in October was 2.3. In February, the class grade-level average was 3.3. There had been a year's growth in just four months! When the final assessment was given, the class grade-level average was 4.9, more than double at the beginning of the year. From October to May, the class average was 2.6 years growth, which paralleled Griffith's data. Growth was also reflected on the Stanford Reading Test that was given in April. On average, the class had grown 2 years, or grade levels, according to Stanford scores.

In year two, student growth was measured with the Stanford 10. Their baseline scores were taken from the end of first grade. The average gain from January to March was 20 percentile points.

Conclusion

What started out as a three-year action research project is now in its fourth year. Michelle is once again a reading coach. "Now I am trying to turn even more teachers on to Readers Theater and fluency practice," she says. She continues to conduct workshops and demonstrate fluency lessons in classrooms.

In addition to getting more classrooms involved in fluency instruction, Michelle wants to continue her action research so that she has data to show it makes a difference. Recently, she received approval for a fluency project that will involve working with fourth-grade struggling readers in collaboration with the reading intervention teacher. Once again, she will follow Griffith's research plan, beginning this year with Readers Theater. She wants to gather data with this group "just to prove how it helps all readers, no matter the grade." Michelle will also create a fluency newsletter for teachers, talking about the "whys" and "hows" of fluency instruction.

One professional article set Michelle White on the road to teacher research and she helped many students, parents, and teachers understand the significance (and fun!) of reading fluency.

Reflections

1. When was the last time you heard someone use the term *scientifically based reading research*? How do you feel when you hear that term?

2. Have you ever conducted research in your own classroom? Describe what you did and the results that you obtained.

3. What research have you read that you could duplicate?

4. What are the barriers to conducting action research?

5. How can the barriers be overcome?

6. Think about reading fluency in your classroom. What do you wonder about? Write three questions that could be answered by teacher action research.

Word Recognition Leads to Fluency

in Indianapolis

When students cannot read most of the words in a text, they cannot read fluently. Approximately 95 percent word recognition is considered adequate for instructional-level reading. Fluent readers recognize most words automatically. The significance of achieving automaticity is that readers can devote their limited cognitive resources to the important task of comprehending the text (LaBerge & Samuels, 1974).

A common strategy for teaching word recognition is the word wall, where words are listed alphabetically and are always visible for reading practice or to be used as a reference when writing. Many classrooms have two separate word walls. One wall displays high-frequency words, and the other displays vocabulary words from literature or content area studies in which the students are currently engaged.

One easy-to-implement and effective strategy for building word recognition fluency is known as the "hotel bell" strategy; it makes word wall words a part of students' everyday vocabulary rather than just a resource they can refer to when they are in school. All you need is a bell like the ones that sit on counters of hotels or small shops. When a word from the word wall is used in an authentic context, someone rings the bell. The hotel bell strategy works well with both types of word walls described above and provides an incentive for students to use these words in their written and oral language.

The Hotel Bell Strategy

Every time she hears the hotel bell ding, second-grade teacher Cheryl McBride gets excited. "They are becoming so interested in words!" she says about her students. "And if they are learning more words, then they will become better readers. It's working!"

Cheryl had taken three years away from teaching to begin a family. One of the first things she did when she returned to teaching was to attend a reading conference to refresh her skills. There, she heard Timothy Rasinski speak about fluency instruction. technique for fluency. Cheryl shares:

Fluency was new for me coming back. When I came out of college in the 1980s we were big into reading groups. Then the whole language movement came along and we inched away from scripted teachers' manuals. Now I was coming back to a more structured environment again. However, Tim talked about things I remembered doing when I was a student—singing and poetry—and I don't think teachers have been doing these things for a while. It made me think of a poem I learned when I was in second grade. I can still recite it even though I usually have a really poor memory. I remember singing songs in school. I said, "Oh my gosh. This is stuff I did when I was in school.

During her 17 years as an educator, Cheryl has attended many, many staff development sessions. She often came home excited but quickly became frustrated because she had heard so much and become overwhelmed trying to implement all of it right away. "Now I am determined to pick one or two things and do those well," she says. The one thing she picked from Rasinski's session was the hotel bell idea. Cheryl wanted to implement the strategy—as soon as she found a bell at an office-supply store. Cheryl reasons:

We had a word wall with interesting words, but all we did was read the words, talk about the definition, and then a few days later, we'd move on to another set. The words were just sitting there, and nobody was using them. After hearing Tim speak about fluency, I saw the bell as a way to help my students become more fluent readers by learning to read more words automatically."

The Hotel Bell Lesson Plan

Before introducing the bell, Cheryl and her students had a conversation about what makes a good reader. The students gave answers that are typical when students are asked what makes a good reader: *Good readers know all the words. Good readers read fast. Good readers read hard books.* Cheryl took this opportunity to discuss fluency with her students. She told them:

Reading fast doesn't always mean someone is a good reader. The important thing is that you really understand what you are reading. When you read fluently, you understand better. Fluency is partly reading at a good speed, but it's more like reading smoothly rather than racing. Fluency also means using expression. But you can't do all this if you don't know the words in the first place, so we are going to be doing something that will help you know more words so that you can be a fluent reader.

Cheryl then explained to her second graders how the hotel bell project would work. Each day, she would put the bell on someone's desk until every student had a turn, and then they would start over. When the "bell dinger" heard one of the word wall words used in conversation, he or she would hit the bell. Suddenly, not only were students listening for the words to see if the bell dinger would catch it, but they were intentionally using the words so that the bell would ring.

Not surprisingly, it didn't take long for the novelty of the bell to motivate students. Within two hours on the first day, Cheryl took down a few words (boring, quickly, calm) because they were being overused! Soon, however, students settled into the game and began using words that were not in their everyday vocabulary—words like *amazement, overjoyed, trudged,* and *toppled.* "What impressed me most was, all of a sudden, they were looking at the word wall," Cheryl says.

Improving the Hotel Bell Strategy

An important addition to the hotel bell activity is that students are frequently asked to select words for the word wall. Recently, they were reading *Chicken Sunday* (Polacco, 1992). They decided to add *solemn, intricate, solo,* and *splendid* to the word wall. *Splendid* words for eight-year-olds, indeed!

Cheryl is considering how to make this strategy even more effective. Sometimes students "gather around" a few of the more common words, like *calm, finally, eager, quickly,* and *boring.*

> One of the challenges for me is to get them using what Tim calls Tier 2 words. They are not in a child's everyday language, but they're also not esoteric. I want them to start focusing on words that are harder to use in conversation, like *adventure, invincible, intricate.*

Cheryl is considering rewarding students when they focus on Tier 2 words (such as *bristled* or *wondrous*) that have not been used. (See pages 53–54.) She currently has an award program for behavior where she gives students a paper bone (to go with the school mascot). When they collect 10 bones they get to eat lunch with Cheryl. This is very popular, and Cheryl thinks it might work to encourage even more vocabulary growth.

Recently, "just for the heck of it," Cheryl gave each student a word from the word wall and asked them to use it in a sentence. Some of the words were *stubborn, huddled, toppled, patient,* and *flicked.* Sentences included: "My brother toppled off the bed"; "I huddled in the corner"; "I was very patient in the doctor's office" (which provided a teachable moment about wordplay). Cheryl was especially pleased when one of the lowest readers in the class used the sentence, "I flicked a crumb off the table at lunch." She has decided she will do this activity from time to time to focus students on the more difficult words.

Evidence of Success

Cheryl thought the excitement might wear off, but the hotel bell continues to engage students with words. She observes, "With very little effort on my part, they are trying to use words in conversation. They're always listening." Sometimes the bell dinger misses a word and other students verbally make a "ding" sound. Sometimes Cheryl says a word without realizing it and students immediately let her know. Sometimes during DEAR (Drop Everything and Read), students encounter a word wall word and take the book to Cheryl and point it out, thus confirming for Cheryl that the hotel bell is helping her students develop automaticity in word recognition, a necessary component of fluency.

One day, Shala, a struggling reader, spotted a word on her Scholastic book order form. She couldn't read the word, but she knew it matched one on the word wall. She asked another student to read it for her. Cheryl says, "Even though she can't read the word yet, she can match it in one-to-one correspondence, and that's the first step."

During the district benchmarking tests, the bell was silenced in Cheryl's desk drawer. It was almost comical to hear students softly making a "ding" sound as they encountered some of the words that had now become part of their lexicon.

The students began applying what they learned in real-life contexts and told Cheryl when they used some of the words at home. Ja'Quan said, "I told my sister, 'KeKe, I'm glaring at you!'" Holly reported that she told her mother about the hotel bell and how she was learning to read more words from the word wall. She said, "I used the word *quickly* in a sentence and my mom and I both said, 'Ding!' My dad thought we were both crazy."

One evening, not finding what she wanted to eat, Brey announced to her family, "There is barely any food in this refrigerator!" At one time she would have said, "There's no food here," but the new word wall word *barely* made her comment more colorful.

One day, Terrell used a word from the word wall in context and then said "ding" to herself. When her mom questioned her, she patiently reminded her of what she had been told at parent conferences about the word wall.

Conclusion

Cheryl has seen the benefit of the hotel bell in increasing oral and listening vocabulary. She is convinced that this vocabulary growth will result in better readers—readers who love words, are fluent, and comprehend what they read. Cheryl sums it up:

> They are learning some authentic things. It's in real conversation. What makes my heart happiest is if Ja'Quan spends all day trying to get *eager* into a sentence, and then he goes home and gets it into a conversation at dinner. Then I'm excited. It's a very powerful thing and he's doing it on his own. Yeah!

Reflections

1. Do you have a word wall? What strategies do you use to encourage students to use the words in their everyday conversation and writing?

2. Do you ever have students who are unwilling to try unknown words? What do you do? What else could you try?

3. Do you ever have students who seem to recognize most of the words but are still not fluent readers? What do you think they need?

4. How many of your students regularly work at an instructional level (92–98 percent accuracy in word recognition)? Does it vary by subject?

5. How do you teach word recognition? After reading this chapter, is there anything you might do differently?

6. How else might you draw students' attention to the words you want them to learn?

The 100 Most Frequently Used Words

A		B	C	D E	
a about all an	and are as at	be been but by	call can come could	day did do down	each

F G		H		I J		K L
find first for from	get go	had has have he	her him his how	I if in into	is it its	like long look

M N	O	P Q R	S
made make many may more my no not now number	of on one or other out	part people put	said see she so some

T	U V	W X	Y Z
than that the their then them there these they this time to two	up use	was water way we were what when which who will with word would write	you your

Source: Literacy for the 21st Century: A Balanced Approach; by G. F. Tompkins, 2006.

100 High-Frequency Words for Older Students

A	B	C	D	E
a lot again all right although another anything around	beautiful because belief beneath between board/bored breathe brought	caught certain close/clothes committee complete	decided desert dessert different discussed doesn't	either embarrassed enough especially etcetera everything everywhere excellent experience
F G	**H**	**I J**	**K L**	**M N O**
familiar favorite field finally foreign friends frighten	hear/here heard/herd height herself himself humorous hungry	immediately interesting its/it's	knew-new know-no knowledge language lying	maybe necessary neighbor once ourselves
P	**Q R**	**R**	**S**	**T**
particular peace/piece people please possible probably	quiet quite	really receive recommend remember restaurant right/write	safety school separate serious since something special success	their/they're/ there themselves though thought threw/through throughout to/two/too together
U V	**W**	**X Y Z**		
until usually	weight were/we're where whether whole/hole	your/you're		

Source: Literacy for the 21st Century: A Balanced Approach; by G. F. Tompkins, 2006.

Closing the Achievement Gap
in Lebanon, Indiana

Several children are standing on the school stage, scripts in hand. There are no props, no costumes, no special lighting, and no memorized lines. They begin to read aloud, and suddenly the audience is totally engaged in a story that comes to life as the children use their voices to create the setting and develop their characters. Another successful Readers Theater performance has begun!

Readers Theater, first popular in colleges and universities, has now become a successful instructional strategy in elementary classrooms. Students usually perform in their own classroom, for parents or as part of a school program, for younger students, or for other classes. Regardless of the audience, the repeated reading practice before a performance is an important factor in building fluency. In addition, Readers Theater can enhance listening and speaking skills, and improve students' confidence.

Readers Theater scripts are typically based on poems, familiar books, or traditional stories. Scripts for social studies and science are also quite popular. There are thousands of ready-made scripts available through commercial publishers and free on the Internet. In addition, many teachers have students create their own scripts from classroom literature as a way of incorporating writing skills. It's a strategy with big returns for very little preparation time on the part of teachers.

Readers Theater in the Classroom

Destiny looked intently at the audience and cleared her throat. Then, with confidence and perfect pronunciation, she began to read the script in her hand:

"The Three Billy Goats Gruff: A Norwegian Folktale. Once upon a time there were three billy goats who wanted to go up to the hillside to make themselves fat. The name of all three was Gruff."

55

Destiny paused and looked toward James, a fellow student. James grinned mischievously and started to read his part.

"On the way up was a bridge. And under the bridge lived a great ugly troll, with eyes as big as saucers and a nose as long as a poker."

James widened his eyes and made a facial contortion that would scare the bravest of billy goats. Immediately, he burst into uncontrollable giggles. Suddenly, 23 third-grade students were laughing hysterically along with James.

"Cut," Mrs. Howe said, laughing. "James, that's a great addition to the script. Let's see if you can do it again, but this time, try to hold the laughter so you really look like a fierce troll."

The six students continued with their first Readers Theater performance and the audience began chiming in with "Trip, trap, trip, trap, trip trap." At the conclusion of their performance, the readers took a bow to much applause and put their scripts back into their Readers Theater folders.

Mrs. Howe heard pleas from all over the room. "Can we go next? Can we go next?" Ah, Readers Theater! She had found something that engaged her students, especially the struggling readers.

Pam Howe teaches third grade in a school with a large number of students who live in poverty. Teachers there, like their counterparts in similar schools across the country, hear the phrase "closing the achievement gap" a lot. Also, as in similar schools, they face the pressure to improve test scores. Pam's principal, Kelly Sollman, and the teachers at Hattie B. Stokes Elementary School are committed to closing that gap, not just to improve test scores, but also to assure that their students will have the opportunity to live happy and productive lives.

During her first year of teaching, Pam tried a number of instructional strategies to improve reading achievement. She saw some success, but she wanted more. "At the end of that year, I went to a workshop with Tim Rasinski. I realized that my kids were having problems with fluency. Their reading was choppy, and because of that, they weren't comprehending." As a new teacher, Pam was uncertain how to get Readers Theater started, so she asked the district reading director, Suzi Boyett, to meet with her. Together they created a plan for implementing Readers Theater in Pam's classroom.

In the fall, as Pam began her second year of teaching, Suzi visited the classroom and did Readers Theater lessons as Pam watched. Then the two of them team-taught some Readers Theater lessons. It wasn't long before Pam and her class were in full swing. As of this writing, Pam is in her third year of teaching and continues to improve upon what she and her students do with Readers Theater.

Readers Theater Lesson Plan

Because many of Pam's students are not fluent readers, she decided this year to begin Readers Theater only after students became comfortable with reading aloud. They spent several weeks choral-reading poetry and singing songs that Pam displayed on the overhead projector. Oral reading as a group helped the reluctant readers to gain confidence before they had to read aloud by themselves. Pam explains, "We talked about expression, rate, and intonation. When their fluency began improving, we moved slowly into Readers Theater." Pam believes students also felt more confident with Readers Theater because she started with scripts from stories that many of the students knew. "They like that. They are more motivated," she says.

The class does Readers Theater every week, with scripts from *Readers Theater for Building Fluency* (Worthy, 2005) and free scripts Pam downloads from the Internet. (See sources on page 58). Together, Pam and her students choose five scripts, then groups are formed to work with each script. Students are not grouped by ability, but Pam tries to steer the lower-level readers toward first- and second-grade materials. She recognizes that they can handle more difficult materials—they simply need more support and more opportunities to practice to reach a level at which they are proficient.

Pam says that Friday is the day everyone looks forward to:

> Performance is a big day. Because they don't have to memorize their scripts, they can get creative. They love to use their voices. For example, if someone has the part of a bear, he might try to sound growly like a bear. They really love it.

Readers Theater Routine

Each day begins with 15 minutes of Readers Theater following the plan below:

Monday: Scripts are chosen and parts are assigned.

Tuesday: Students read through the scripts to become familiar with the story line and vocabulary.

Wednesday: Each group reads through its script again, concentrating on expression, rate, and intonation.

Thursday: Students read through the scripts once again, this time practicing for the performance with a special emphasis on projection.

Friday: Each group performs. Usually they perform within the classroom, but occasionally they perform for other classrooms.

The following Monday, the students begin the same instructional cycle with new materials that will be performed the following Friday.

Evidence of Success

Pam believes Readers Theater helps to close the achievement gap within her classroom, she explains:

> Some of the kids went up several reading levels. The children are much more comfortable with reading aloud, and they are reading more fluently, which helps their comprehension. What's really good is that Readers Theater transfers. They are excited to read to me in reading groups. They want to read aloud their writing, too. Some parents have commented that when their kids read aloud, they hear them reading words the kids didn't know before.

10 Sources for Readers Theater Scripts

Barchers, S. I. (2003). *Readers theatre for beginning readers.* Portsmouth, NH: Teacher Ideas Press.

Clark, S. K. (2007). *Reader's theater scripts, grade 5.* Huntington Beach, CA: Shell Educational.

Fredericks, A. D. (2007). *Mother Goose readers theatre for beginning readers.* Portsmouth, NH: Teacher Ideas Press.

Fredericks, A. D. (2007). *Nonfiction readers theatre for beginning readers.* Portsmouth, NH: Teacher Ideas Press.

Freeman, J. (2007). *Once upon a time: Using storytelling, creative drama, and readers theater with children in grades pre-K-6.* Portsmouth, NH: Libraries Unlimited.

McGee, B. & McGee, T. (2007). *Readers theater and so much more!* Waco, TX: Prufrock Press.

Ratliff, G. L. (1999). *Introduction to readers theatre: A guide to classroom performance.* Colorado Springs, CO: Meriwether Publishing.

Roper, A., Sishton, E., Farley, J. & Coleman, M. (2001). *Readers' theater, level 1.* Lindon, UT: Instructional Fair.

Sloyer, S. (2003). *From the page to the stage: The educator's complete guide to readers theatre.* Portsmouth, NH: Teacher Ideas Press.

Worthy, J. (2005). *Readers theater for building fluency: Strategies and scripts for making the most of this highly effective, motivating, and research-based approach to oral reading.* Monterey, CA: Evan-Moor.

From January through March, 10 of Pam's 23 students increased their reading achievement by two grade levels, a fact she attributes to Readers Theater. "Of course, we can't say definitely that Readers Theater is the entire cause," Pam admits, "but the other classes at my grade level only saw half that amount of gain."

Some of Pam's colleagues have heard about what is happening in third grade and have asked how they can get started. The school staff works in Professional Learning Communities (PLC) and that has provided a context for Pam to share. "I brought some scripts to PLC and showed them how I got started. Some teachers are now using my overheads of poetry and songs to get started."

Conclusion

More and more students are finding success in Lebanon, Indiana's Readers Theater. "Trip, trap, trip, trap, trip, trap! Who's that walking on my bridge?" It's Pam Howe and her third graders—trip-trapping off to close the achievement gap.

Reflections

1. What are the differences and similarities between a classroom play and Readers Theater? What are the advantages and disadvantages of each?

2. Is repeated reading important for normally developing and advanced readers, or is it simply an "extra" for them?

3. What skills could you model using a Readers Theater script?

4. What is one science concept you teach that would lend itself to a Readers Theater script?

5. What would you do if a student did not want to participate in Readers Theater? How would you encourage this student to give it a try? What are the motivating forces in Readers Theater?

Readers Theater Script:

The Three Billy Goats Gruff

Roles

Little Billy Goat Gruff	Big Billy Goat Gruff	Narrator 1
Middle Billy Goat Gruff	Troll	Narrator 2

Narrator 1: Welcome to our show. Today's play is "The Three Billy Goats Gruff."

Narrator 2: As Little Billy Goat Gruff strolls through the fields, he sees a rickety, old bridge. On the other side of the bridge is a meadow with green, green grass and apple trees.

Little BGG: I'm the littlest billy goat. I have two big brothers. I want to go across this bridge to eat some green, green grass and apples so that I can be big like my two brothers.

Narrator 1: Little Billy Goat Gruff starts across the bridge.

All: *(softly)* Trip, trap, trip, trap, trip, trap.

Narrator 2: Just as Little Billy Goat Gruff comes to the middle of the bridge, an old troll pops up from underneath.

Troll: Who is that walking on my bridge? (Snort, snort!)

Source: Galdone, P. (1981). *The Three Bill Goats Gruff.* (timelessteacherstuff.com)

Little BGG: It's only me, Little Billy Goat Gruff.

Troll: Arrrgh! I'm a big, bad troll and you are on *my* bridge. I'm going to eat you for my breakfast. *(Snort, snort!)*

Little BGG: I just want to eat some green, green grass and apples in the meadow. Please don't eat me, Mister Troll. I'm just a little billy goat. Wait until my brother comes along. He is much bigger and tastier than me.

Troll: Bigger? Tastier? Well, all right. I guess I will. Go ahead and cross the bridge. Arrrgh.

Little BGG: Thank you very much, you great big, ugly old troll.

Troll: What did you call me? Come back here! Grrrr!"

Little BGG: Bye!

All: *(softly)*   "Trip, trap, trip, trap, trip, trap."

Narrator 1:   Little Billy Goat Gruff ran across the bridge. He ate the green, green grass and apples. The troll went back under his bridge and went to sleep.

Narrator 2:   Before long, Middle-Size Billy Goat Gruff walks up to the rickety, old bridge. He, too, sees the meadow with the green, green grass and apple trees.

Middle-Size BGG: I'm the middle-size billy goat. I have a big brother and a little brother. I want to go across this bridge to eat some green, green grass and apples so that I can be big like my brother.

Narrator 1:   Middle-Size Billy Goat Gruff starts across the bridge.

All: *(middle-sized voice)* Trip, trap, trip, trap, trip, trap.

Narrator 2:   Just as the Middle-Size Billy Goat Gruff comes to the middle of the bridge, the old troll pops up from underneath.

Troll: Grrr. Who is that walking on my bridge? Arrgh!

Middle-Size BGG: It is I, Middle-Size Billy Goat Gruff.

Troll: Arrgh! I'm a big, bad troll and you are on my bridge. I'm going to eat you for my lunch. Snort, snort!

Middle-Size BGG: I just want to eat some green, green grass and apples in the meadow. Please don't eat me, Mister Troll. I'm just a middle-size billy goat. Wait until my brother comes along. He is much bigger and much, much tastier than I am.

Troll: Bigger? Tastier? Hmm. All right, I guess I will. Go ahead and cross the bridge.

Middle-Size BGG: Thank you very much, you great big, really ugly and dirty old troll.

Troll: What did you call me? Grrrr. Come back here right this very instant!

Middle BGG: Oh, nothing. See ya!

All: *(a bit louder)*   Trip, trap, trip, trap, trip, trap.

Narrator 1:   Middle-Size Billy Goat Gruff ran across the bridge. He ate the green, green grass and apples. The troll went back under his bridge and once again fell fast sleep.

Narrator 2:   After a while, Big Billy Goat Gruff sees the rickety, old bridge. On the other side of the bridge is a meadow with green, green grass and apple trees.

Big BGG: I'm the biggest billy goat. I have two brothers. I want to go across this bridge to eat some green, green grass and apples just as they did.

Narrator 1:   So Big Billy Goat Gruff starts across the bridge.

All: (louder)   Trip, trap, trip, trap, trip, trap!

Narrator 2:   Just as Big Billy Goat Gruff got to the middle of the bridge, an old troll pops up from underneath

Troll: Grrr. Who is that walking on my bridge?

Big BGG: It is I, Big Billy Goat Gruff.

Troll: Grrrr. I'm a big, bad troll and you are on my bridge. I'm going to eat you for my supper. Snort, snort!

Big BGG: Really? (smiles at audience) Well, come right on up here and have a feast then. (grins at audience)

Narrator 1:   The troll climbs onto the bridge. Big Billy Goat Gruff lowers his head and charges the troll! Big Billy Goat Gruff knocks the troll clean off the bridge and into the icy cold water!

Troll: Glug, glug, glug. Grrr. Grrr. Brrr. Brrr.

Big BGG: Brothers, that ugly old bully won't bother us again. I butted him with my horns and knocked him off the bridge and into the icy cold water. I've done my job, and from now on we can come and go in peace. Now, I'm going to go and eat some of that green, green grass and some apples.

All: *(Loud)*   Trip, trap, trip, trap, trip, trap!

Narrator 2:   Big Billy Goat Gruff crosses the bridge and joins his brothers. He eats the green, green grass and apples.

Little Billy Goat: Munch, munch, munch.

Little and Middle-Size Billy Goat: Munch, munch, munch.

All Three Billy Goats: Munch, munch, munch. This green, green grass is great for lunch!

Narrator 1:   And that mean, ugly, old troll? He never came back to the bridge. He learned that being mean never pays.

Troll: This water feels like ice. Brrr, brrr, brrr. Next time, I'll try being nice!

All: The End!

A High-Tech Poetry Carnival

in Lafayette, California

Giving students an opportunity to listen to and assess their own oral reading by means of digital technology is one of the many exciting thresholds being crossed in the realm of fluency instruction (Johnston, 2006). Voice print technology, which was once confined to expensive oscilloscopes in remote labs, can now be found on nearly all networked computers, giving learners a chance to see what they are saying. Since "any child likes to hear his or her own voice!" (Johnston, p. 130), activities that give students chances to record and listen to themselves are both motivating and metacognitive. The technology allows immediate feedback, so that students can improve upon their previous performance right away—and they often wish to do so!

That is what Sue Park found with third graders in the low reading group at her school when she developed this fluency-centered project. Sue's commitment to fine children's poetry, student writing, and fluency instruction, combined with her confidence in using the school's available technology, resulted in a winning combination. The integrated, weeklong project combines many features found in best classroom practices, and the results of Sue's action research would make any teacher proud. The fluency project allows students to choose their own poems from within a range of readable texts, practice repeated reading in pairs, and use their neglected multiple intelligences through drawing, writing, reading, listening, and performing a poem. What's more, students' reading comprehension rates have risen!

The Animal Poetry Project

"It's so it tiring to hear children read in monotones!" Sue Park agreed with this oft-repeated teacher comment, wanted to do something about it, and knew that, for some learners, "seeing is believing." Fortunately, inexpensive and user-friendly technology has enabled Sue to find unique ways to effectively enhance her classes' fluency instruction.

Lafayette Elementary School, a Title I School in Lafayette, California, where Park works, uses a tiered reading program for third grade. This is the grade the school considers to be "critical to cement reading skills." Designed to target individual reading needs, the program has students "travel" with their reading group one hour a day for five-week units. For the last four years, Sue has instructed the students with the lowest reading levels, and she focuses on building reading fluency and comprehension.

Sue is a true believer in using fluency instruction in her classroom. She uses the Read Naturally program (readnaturally.com), Readers Theater (she finds the scripts at ReadingA-z.com), choral poetry, and other techniques she learned studying at St. Mary's College of California under Professor Mary Kay Moskal (Moskal & Blachowicz, 2006). She finds fluency to be the most effective and enjoyable way to send her students on to fourth grade not only enjoying reading, but meeting at grade-level benchmarks.

Sue's Animal Poetry project introduces several brand-new elements. Students choose a poem, practice it, write about why they chose it, and read the poetry expressively into a recording device. As they practice, they look at voice imaging software that allows them to see the difference between how expressive reading "looks" compared to reading in a monotone. After seeing the teacher's own voice print when reading in a monotone, and then expressively, they can compare their own vocal modulation and have a chance to modify their recordings until their voice print looks expressive,

and sounds that way as well. Each child then creates a drawing of the animal in the poem he or she has chosen to perform. Sue uploads the recorded poems at the school website in the form of a podcast, and uploads their accompanying animal drawings, which can then be viewed by the students and the school community. A real production!

The Animal Poetry Podcast Lesson Plan

The groups meet one hour a day for five weeks, and the Animal Poetry Podcast project is spread out over one week, not counting Sue's preparation before the project, time the children spend practicing the poems at home, and the additional time Sue needs to upload the sound and graphics files. She says that each time the technical features get a little easier. Here is the way Sue organizes the project before, during, and after the recordings are made.

Before the Project

* Sue selects several books of animal poetry, at three or more different reading levels. Douglas Florian's animal poetry books (2002, 2005), the poetry of Shel Silverstein (1974, 1993, 2002), and Jack Prelutsky's poems (2002, 2006) are especially good choices. Sue recommends that at least one of the books have shorter poems with more common vocabulary, such as Shel Silverstein's poems "Early Bird" (1974, p. 30) or "Toucan" (p. 92), each just four lines long.

* Before starting the unit, Sue records herself reading one of the poems, using Apple GarageBand program. GarageBand shows the dynamics of the vocal performance. She reads the poem in a monotone the first time through, and the second time, she reads the same poem expressively. Sue does this simply by plugging a microphone into her Mac. She saves the voice files to her computer so they can be played back for the children in class. These two recordings can be used in the future, with new classes.

* Sue sends home a note telling families that the children are going to record poetry and that their performances will be published on a website.

During the Project

The first day of the project, Sue introduces the idea that students will be choosing a poem, illustrating it, writing about their chosen poem, practicing it, and then recording it for publication on to the Internet.

* Sue plays her two recorded samples for the students, using an LCD projector hooked up to her computer, to show them the difference in the appearance of the voice for the two performances of the poem. More dynamic, expressive speaking can immediately be identified by its wider voice print, whereas

the monotonous reading shows a flat voice print. Showing students a visual representation of expressive reading with the voice imaging software gives them a great tool to guide their own performances.

* She helps all of the students choose an animal poem of their own, at their instructional level. Making sure the text is at the correct level for a student's current proficiency is key. Says Sue, "I target reading levels for almost every fluency activity." For this project, "we read samples from about four books and talked about picking something 'just right'—not too long, but not too short—and using words they felt comfortable with."

* Once they choose their poems, students practice repeatedly reading them with a partner, on several different days.

* Sue makes copies of each student's poem, so that they can take the poems home to practice with their families.

* Students write about why they have chosen their particular poem. They are told that this piece of writing will be recorded as the introduction to their poem. They practice reading their own writing to their partners.

* Students study their individual animal poems, underlining the words they plan to emphasize in their reading performance, and talk with Sue about why they have chosen those words. This part of the lesson insures that comprehension of the poem, not just its performance, is part of the unit.

* After students have practiced the poems in pairs on several days, they draw a penciled sketch of the animal featured in their poem.

* On performance day, all students take their poems and sketches to the computer lab, where the recordings take place. The children take turns recording their poem in one corner of the lab. While one student is recording, the next in line warms up by rehearsing the poem with Sue's teaching assistant outside the lab.

* After each recording, Sue replays the performance so that students can hear their voices and see how their vocal expression looks on the voice imaging software. The voice prints fascinate everyone and give the enterprise a "scientific" feel. If they want to rerecord it, they can—and several do. The difference in expressiveness is dramatic when this tool is available.

* While waiting their turn to be recorded, children fill in their drawings of their poem's animal, using Broderbund's Kid Pix Deluxe program. "Everyone has plenty to do as they await their turn to record," Sue says. "It takes us two and a half reading sessions to pick the poem, practice, record, and make our pictures." When waiting for their turn, "students also get a bit of phonics work in while sitting at the computers—so they keep busy."

✷ After school, Sue combines the students' art with their audio performance and uploads them both to her class website, which parents can view with a password.

Launching the Website

The podcast of the student performances was made available at the school website, and was shown at the parent open house. It garnered enthusiastic feedback from parents and children alike. Not only that, Sue's project combines many of the features that are proven to work in best practice fluency instruction: student choice, modeling by an expert other, opportunities to do repeated reading, a performance component, and a chance for self-monitoring (Rasinski, Blachowicz & Lems, 2006). Even better, Sue builds student writing and art into the project, and showcases them using simple and affordable technology. All of these factors contribute to the success of the Animal Poetry project.

The Technology

Sue successfully uses available technology to create and enhance this experience. Because she is on Lafayette's technology committee, she has become familiar with how to incorporate new technologies in the classroom. However, she insists that anything in the project can be done by a classroom teacher with a bit of know-how and practice. Here is the terminology and technology needed for a podcast project like this.

✷ **Podcasting** allows audio or video files to be saved on the Internet and made available for viewing at a time of the listener's choosing, through the click of a button. This is available as a free download through many servers. With YouTube technology, it is now easy to save videos as podcasts, too.

✷ **Apple's GarageBand** is an immensely popular free audio mixing board and recording studio that works on any Apple Macintosh computer. It works like a small recording studio. Users can select a wide variety of instrument sounds, consider possible orchestral arrangements, adjust sound quality, and save what they have created. Recording speaking voices is a simple matter and requires only a microphone, something all Apple computers have.

✷ **Kid Pix Deluxe** is a drawing program from Broderbund for which Sue's school has a site license. Among other things, it allows children to draw pictures that are saved to a computer and can be projected or transferred to a number of platforms. It allows Sue to connect pictures drawn by the children to their audio files. She notes that, lacking this software, if a

69

scanner is available, students can make simple drawings with markers on paper, then have them scanned and saved to the computer. The charming drawings created for this project enhance the poetry performances by giving listeners something to engage them visually as they listen to the poetry. It also makes students less self-conscious since it takes some of the audience focus off their vocal performance.

✳ **Quicktime** is a free downloadable software program that allows the students' audio and video work to be played on any computer screen. This is one of many free software programs that plays music and video images. It can be used on both Mac computers and PCs, and it comes loaded on many computers. It is possible to access an example of the poetry performances of Sue's class using Quicktime Media at the website listed in the references (Park, 2010).

✳ **One or more external microphones** are needed, so that the students with softer voices can be recorded audibly. The microphones need to be plugged into one of the computer's port jacks. Although most computers now have built-in microphones, the quality is not satisfactory for a vocal recording in a fluency-focused project, in which expressive reading is so central. If unsure about which kind of equipment to use, check with the people who maintain the equipment in the school computer lab. Inexpensive microphones can be bought at electronics stores and through online computer accessory suppliers.

✳ **Access to a secure website** is needed, so performances can be viewed at a later time. Many schools or districts have these, and they often include locations at which teachers can upload their class projects.

Evidence of Success

Fluency tracking done in September and February of their third-grade year showed tremendous gains for all the children in the project, and 4 of the 20 children moved out of the lowest group by February. "Most everybody was at benchmark by the end of the year," says Sue. "This project is a great showcase for our struggling readers."

The growth of the Sue's third-grade low reading group was determined according to two measures: the Slosson Oral Reading Test (SORT, slosson.com, 2009), which provides a quick glance at students' word recognition; and the well-known Dynamic Indicators of Basic Early Literacy Skills, (DIBELS), a reading test designed to be administered three times each year from kindergarten through third grade (DIBELS/uoregon.edu, 2010). In Sue's school, children reading below 70 words correct per minute at the start of third grade receive this fluency instruction, with a goal of reaching the spring benchmark of 110 words correct per minute by the end of third grade. "Half of the children are over or almost at the benchmark as a result of our intervention program. And everyone grew in fluency," she says.

Conclusion

Sue is doing her fluency project for a second year now, and it's going very well. But don't take it on faith—see and hear for yourself by visiting her website, "Welcome to Our Podcast!" (Park, 2007). Sue beams, "In a survey about their overall fluency instruction, students were most proud of their poetry podcast."

Reflections

1. Sue's fluency project includes student art, writing, reading aloud, and performing. In what other kinds of projects could these be combined?

2. What are some other popular children's poems that might work well for a project like this? What other themes could be chosen for the poetry and art?

3. A lot of children are experimenting with musical and rhythmic tracks they find in simple software and keyboards. How could such rhythm tracks be used as a backup sound to reading poetry?

4. How could this project be adapted to video rather than audio?

5. Some teachers create projects in other software, such as Microsoft's PowerPoint or Movie Maker. Thinking about the technology you know, what parts of this fluency project could you implement with what you already know? What new things would you need to learn?

6. There is a 14-part symphony called "Carnival of the Animals" by the French composer Camille Saint-Saëns. Each part features a different animal through a musical theme. How could those pieces be added to Sue's class project? Try to think of other songs or works of classical music that could be added to collections of poetry on different themes.

Repeated Reading Success
in Harford County, Maryland

Repeated reading is a fluency strategy that's well established in the research literature. Endorsed by the National Reading Panel (2000), it has been shown to be effective in improving reading achievement (Rasinski & Hoffman, 2003; Samuels, 1979). In repeated reading, students are asked to read short passages several times until they achieve a level of fluent reading. Common sense tells us that when students engage in repeated readings, they naturally improve on the passage they are practicing—allowing them to move on to texts of equal or greater difficulty. A more surprising, and exciting, finding is that students also improve on passages they have not previously read (Rasinski & Hoffman, 2003; Rasinski, Padak, Linek & Sturtevant, 1994; Samuels, 1979; Stahl & Heubach, 2005). That's the sometimes elusive "transfer" that signals real learning and growth in reading.

Get Books Into Their Hands

Cathy Bowden is a 30-year veteran teacher and now a full-time mentor for new teachers at Joppatowne and Riverside Elementary Schools. She serves on the School Improvement Team for both schools. Cathy described her schools and the student's reading struggles:

> Our schools are in working-class neighborhoods. We have a wonderful mix of cultures, with 26 percent African American, 3 percent Hispanic, 4 percent Asian, and 67 percent White. Thirty-two percent of our students receive free or reduced lunches, and 15 percent receive special education services. Even so, we fall short of the required number to receive Title I funds from the federal government.

> I work with wonderful, dedicated people who want nothing but the best experiences for the students, but, sometimes lack of money gets in

the way. One day, I was talking about this with Earl Haskins, who is an instructional facilitator for the county. He said, "If only there was some way to get books into the homes of these families. I know that they love their children, but, you know, many of them can't drive to the library or afford to buy quality books on their children's reading levels." Suddenly, I had an idea!

The Family Reading Project

With help and encouragement from principals Chris Cook and Creighton Leizear, Cathy went right to work developing a plan that would become known as the Family Reading Project. She envisioned getting books into children's hands—books they would read, reread, and keep. Cathy presented the idea to her School Improvement Teams and teachers immediately volunteered to help. Committees were formed at both schools, with reading specialists Eleni Constantine and Tracey Weidner cochairing at their respective schools.

Teachers in the schools gave donations and held fund-raisers to help purchase books. They asked local businesses for support and established a community partnership with the Joppatowne Women's Club. At Riverside, additional funds were secured from a special education teacher whose husband owns a local business. Grants were written and funds were regularly received for both schools. The PTAs shared funds or vouchers raised from book fairs.

With adequate funding to "get books into their hands," Cathy then worked with colleagues to establish a process for deciding who should get the books, what they would do with them, and how their progress would be monitored.

Each school surveyed families to find out how many books they had in the home that they considered to be on their child's reading level. In addition, teachers recommended students they felt would benefit most from participation. Teacher nominations were based on data from the Harford Kindergarten Performance Assessment, running records, and scores from the Scholastic Reading Inventory (1999).

Letters were sent to eligible families that told about their children's opportunity to earn books on his or her reading level to read and keep (see page 94).

Excitement was high the day the letters arrived in families' mailboxes. That first year, 94 families accepted the invitation to participate in the Family Reading Project.

Once a family accepted the invitation, information was sent home to help parents understand the important connection between reading with their children and reading achievement. Cathy and her colleagues used newsletters and phone calls to inform parents about the goals, procedures, and benefits of the Family Reading Project. Teachers discussed the project at parent conferences. In addition, Cathy did a presentation on fluency for Reading Night. She talked with parents about the National Reading Panel report (2000) and shared ideas from *The Fluent Reader* (Rasinski, 2003). Cathy and her colleagues also did a workshop for volunteers who read with participating students.

Quality books were purchased through the Scholastic Literacy Partners program because, as Cathy explained, "we found that they gave reduced prices and free shipping to projects qualifying as supporters of family literacy." Students were given books on their reading level and were encouraged to read and reread each book a minimum of five times. Intermediate students read their longer books one time and their favorite part an additional four times for fluency practice. Parents initialed a verification form after a book was read the required number of times and students then earned another new book to keep. Altogether, students returned verification forms for 394 books that year. In the two years the program has been in existence, the two schools have given out more than 1,000 books.

An interesting by-product of the book project at Joppatowne has been a summer reading book giveaway. One of the reading specialists, began getting donations of used books, so she and Cathy approached the principal, Mr. Cook, with the idea of having a book drive to encourage summer reading. He and the committee agreed. Parents and teachers donate gently used books to the project. Each child who participates in the Family Reading Project receives at least 10 books to take home for summer reading. They enjoy choosing books to keep and promise to continue their great efforts.

Evidence of Success

The School Improvement Team at each building has tracked students' progress using the Scholastic Reading Inventory (1999), running records, and pre- and post-reading tests over two years. Students who read and returned ten or more books made significant gains, as evidenced in running records and comprehension tests

Students

Christopher Hinchleff, a second grader, is one of many success stories. His mother reported she was "over the moon" with his progress in reading. Cathy talks about Christopher:

> We were able to catch his interest and he just went wild with reading, when before he showed little motivation or interest. His scores on the Scholastic Reading Inventory went from 25 in the fall to 220 in the spring, with his teacher commenting that his fluency and attitude had greatly improved as well. His teacher, Ashlee Groce, attributed a great deal of his success to his enthusiastic participation in the book project. Christopher's mom commented on her sheet, "He has really bloomed in his reading. His reading has improved 100 percent and he now thinks about expression. I don't think I could get these fantastic results by myself at home. Please continue the project."

Teachers

One hundred percent of teachers surveyed indicated the project was a success. Here are some of their comments:

* This program provided purpose and motivation. My student was proud.

* Please continue the Family Reading Project. It's a great opportunity for students to read books on their level and for parents to read with them.

* My students have a more positive attitude toward reading. Their comprehension improved a noticeable amount.

* My students now keep a book in their hands nearly all the time.

Cathy reports that students' attitudes toward reading improved and their confidence increased. "Eleni, Tracey, and I saw it daily as students came with their verification forms and chose new books to read. They would catch me in the hall and tell me how much they were reading and how excited they were to finish one book and pick another to take home and keep."

Instructional facilitator Connie Tucker reflects:

> When you see students who are engaged readers, you see and feel a new world of energy, because engaged readers want to share their interests and what they are reading with their peers." She adds, "They become more confident and eager to try new strategies in learning how to read. A win-win situation for everyone, especially the children."

Parents

Parents were also very complimentary of the Family Reading Project, with 100 percent who returned surveys indicating they would like to see the project continue and have their children participate again. The parents' comments included the following:

* This project added to my child's enthusiasm for reading.

* It gives children confidence, and my child found it rewarding.

* He is very proud when he can read a book by himself.

* Her reading is getting better. She likes to read to everybody who will let her now. I think it's the best way to get kids to learn.

* My child has developed a continuous positive attitude toward reading. Her reading interest has become almost insatiable. Overall, she reads more fluently, pronounces words better, and reads a lot faster than before. Thank you.

* My son has made a drastic change in his reading. He has more confidence and determination about reading and loves to read to me. I love his enthusiasm about the Family Reading Project.

* My daughter is much more interested in reading. She is now reading on grade level and has so much more confidence. She wants to read.

Conclusion

Cathy and her colleagues are planning ways to engage intermediate students who are not motivated to read and reread long books. They suspect that shorter selections, such as poetry by Shel Silverstein or Jack Prelutsky, might be more motivational. Cathy and other teachers are also considering how they can incorporate Readers Theater scripts (see chapter 13 for more on this fluency strategy) into the Family Reading Project. The plan is to encourage students to practice repeated readings with these kinds of selections, meet biweekly in a "book club" type of meeting to share, and then pair up and share with some of the younger participants.

Repeated reading improves fluency, but first students have to have books in their hands to read. Cathy Bowden and her colleagues in Harford County, Maryland, work tirelessly to make it happen. Cathy summarized it well: "The Family Reading Project sends the message that schools and parents are in this together. It has made a difference. It's quite simple: If their parents read with them, they're going to improve."

Reflections

1. Do you use repeated reading in your classroom? If so, how do you structure it? What materials do you use for repeated reading?

2. Are parents included in your repeated reading efforts?

3. What percentage of your students do you suspect have less than 25 books on their reading level at home?

4. Brainstorm a list of possible resources in your community for helping get books and other reading material into students' hands.

5. What types of texts besides books might work well for repeated readings? Where might you find these texts?

6. What ideas do you have for engaging reluctant older readers in repeated readings?

An Invitation to the Family Reading Project

We are very excited about a reading project we are instituting to increase motivation, achievement, and enthusiasm for reading. The Family Reading Project is designed to allow students opportunities to earn books to read and keep as their own. We are pleased to invite you and your child to be part of this project and we are hopeful that you will join in and enjoy participating. We are hopeful that this project will help our students become more confident, enthusiastic, and able readers.

We believe that by having families model the fun and importance of reading and rereading in the home, it will send the message to students that it is indeed a worthwhile thing to do.

Based on the recent research on how fluency practice positively influences reading progress, we intend to give students free books on their reading level, to read and reread at home. When they have read a book five times, they will be allowed to bring in their ticket documenting their reading from home and will be allowed to choose another quality book (on their reading level) to take home, read, reread, and keep. Simply fill in and return the form

We know that some children need more practice at home than others in order to reinforce classroom instruction and boost reading progress. Your child has been invited to participate because it has been suggested that additional practice at home may benefit his or her reading progress.

Of course, our mission is to provide the most nurturing environment for learning that is possible. We can't do it alone, so we are inviting families to join us in this most important effort. If you accept our invitation, you will be saying yes to spending time with your child reading for fun and enjoyment. Sometimes it is hard to find the time, but we know that by making this commitment, you and your child will be taking a giant step toward improved attitudes and growth in reading. There will be additional information shared so that you will understand and be comfortable with the guidelines of the project. Thanks so much.

Student's Name _____

Teacher _____

_____ *We would like to participate in the Family Reading Project.*

_____ *Thank you for offering, but our family has decided not to participate.*

Parent Signature _____ Date _____

Family Reading Project
Reading for Fluency Verification Form

Name:_____

Teacher:_____

Book Title:_____

Author:_____

I know rereading for fluency helps me become a more confident and able reader.
I have read this book five times to an adult. (If you have read a chapter book, please
document that you have read your favorite part five times, at least 15 minutes of
rereading each time.) I would like to redeem this form for another new book to keep.

Date	Parent or Guardian, please initial
1.	
2.	
3.	
4.	
5.	

When you have completed your verification form, return it to redeem it for your next book. We are glad you are participating in our reading project.

Comments:_____

_____

_____

Teaching to Their Hearts

in Lancaster, Pennsylvania

Echo reading is a fluency strategy in which the teacher reads one section of text aloud with appropriate intonation and phrasing while the student follows along silently in his or her text. The student then reads the same material aloud and tries to match his or her fluency to the model. The process usually starts with one sentence or stanza of a poem. This continues until, over time, the student can imitate more than one sentence or stanza at a time. Research has shown that assisted reading, or reading while listening, is an effective approach for improving students' reading fluency and overall achievement (Chomsky, 1976; National Reading Panel, 2000; Rasinski, 1990).

Echo reading of poetry in the classroom is one of the simplest yet most effective, methods for improving reading fluency.

The teacher reads the poem, leads students in a discussion of the contents of the poem, and then invites them to join him or her in echo reading. Once students have gained fluency, repeated practice of the poem can be varied and fun. Partners can take turns reading stanzas; girls can read some lines and boys read others; students can read some lines loudly and others softly or read several lines in whispers. Some children might write their own version of the poem, then read it aloud to classmates or a partner. The possibilities are endless. And the materials are abundant—from traditional nursery rhymes to the silliness of Shel Silverstein and Jack Prelutsky to the great rhythm and rhyme of Myra Cohn Livingston and Eve Merriam to everyday jump-rope jingles.

No Child Left Without Poetry

Grappling with the recent developments in education—No Child Left Behind, the Individuals with Disabilities Education Improvement Act, Scientifically Based Reading Research, Response to Intervention, Reading First—can be overwhelming. Districts around the country strive valiantly to keep up as acronyms reproduce like rabbits: NCLB, IDEA, SBRR, RTI, etc. How do educators focus on doing what is best for kids?

To bring some of these initiatives down to a practical level, the school district of Lancaster, Pennsylvania invited Timothy Rasinski to do a beginning-of-the-year workshop on fluency. Teachers were excited with what they learned and were convinced of the importance of explicitly teaching fluency to improve reading achievement.

Hambright Elementary teachers were especially receptive, since their high number of struggling readers put them in the test score spotlight. They really liked the idea of including more poetry in the classroom. They purchased copies of *Phonics Poetry: Teaching Word Families* (Rasinski & Zimmerman, 2001) and began writing poems on large chart paper and making copies for the students.

Reading intervention teachers, however, were left by the wayside. In an attempt to meet the needs of struggling readers, the district had purchased materials that were said to be supported by "scientifically based reading research (SBRR)," and those programs did not include poetry.

Sallie Shepherd was one of the teachers who sat in Rasinski's session and dreamed of how fluency could help her students. She is a reading intervention specialist who teaches struggling readers in kindergarten, first, second, and fourth grades. She meets with small groups of students for a half hour each day. Sallie accepts the requirement that she teach the SBRR reading programs to the lowest achievers. However, she explains, "I know that I am responsible for doing these programs, but I couldn't bear just doing the scripts and not putting something of me in it. Fluency is so important. If I can do the required programs and give them something extra, then I want to do that." That "something extra" is poetry.

Sallie has found that she can include poetry in her reading instruction every other day. "I try to stick with it," She says. "If for some reason I don't give them a poem, they sigh a disappointed 'Oh-h-h-h-h.' They want to know why they can't have a poem." Students practice the short, rhythmical texts, focusing on reading accurately and with expression. Children can quickly and easily master the short length, rhyme, and rhythm embedded in poems. Struggling readers feel that they have accomplished something of value in their reading.

Echo Reading of Poetry Lesson Plan

Sallie bases her lessons on the word chunks and vowel patterns (phonograms) that are found in rhymes and poems. Each student has a word study book she or he uses with the poems. Students begin a new poetry lesson by brainstorming words with a vowel sound or pattern Sallie has determined they need to study. For example, recently her second graders worked with the rime *ot*. The students wrote all the *ot* words they could think of in their word study books and then shared them with the large group.

Next, students silently read a poem that contains words with the pattern being studied, in this case *ot* words. They highlight words with the pattern and then add any to their word study book that they did not already have.

Then, Sallie guides the group in echo reading. She first reads the entire poem while students follow along silently. Sallie discusses what she did to read fluently. She tells students why her voice went up or down in certain places, how she read at a nice pace but didn't speed, how she paused at punctuation, or perhaps how she needed to know all the words automatically to make the poem read smoothly. Then Sallie and her students echo-read through the entire poem. Sallie reads one line at a time and the students repeat it, striving to match the pitch, intonation, and speed she uses.

Next, the group reads the poem orally in a variety of formats. They might take turns reading lines, divide the poem by girls and boys, have half the group read the first four lines and the other half read the last four lines, etc. They read the poem "over and over and over," and fluency soon becomes evident.

Each student belongs to the "Lucky Listeners Club" and so receives a copy of the poem to take home and share with family in even more repeated readings at home. Family members who hear the students read the poems sign the Lucky Listener sheet. Sallie reports that many of the students take the packet of poems they have been collecting from the beginning of the year and read every poem every night. One day she asked her students, "What do your parents say? Are they sick of hearing these poems?"

Ryan replied, "No. My mom thinks my reading is good."

Jason smiled and said, "My parents clap when I read to them."

Joel said he liked to do the Lucky Listeners Club because it lets him spend time with his parents.

Recommended Books

For Students

Fleischman, P. (1985). *I am phoenix: Poems for two voices.* New York: Harper Trophy.

Fleischman, P. (1988). *Joyful noise: Poems for two voices.* New York: Harper Trophy.

Harrison, D. L. (2000). *Farmer's garden: Rhymes for two voices.* Honesdale, PA: Boyds Mills.

Hoberman, M. A. (2001). *You read to me, I'll read to you: Very short stories to read together.* New York: Little Brown.

Hoberman, M. A. (2004). *You read to me, I'll read to you: Very short fairy tales to read together.* New York: Little Brown.

Katz, A. (2001). *Take me out of the bathtub: And other silly dilly songs.* New York: Scholastic.

Katz, A. (2003). *I'm still here in the bathtub: Brand new silly dilly songs.* New York: Scholastic.

For Teachers

Kaner, E. (2004). *Word catchers! for reading and spelling.* East Moline, IL: LinguiSystems.

Rasinski, T. V. & Zimmerman, B. S. (2001). *Phonics poetry: Teaching word families.* New York: Allyn & Bacon.

Evidence of Success

The district-adopted programs Sallie teaches include frequent student assessments. Students are timed on words correct per minute as well as on comprehension of the programs' passages. In addition, the district uses DIBELS (Good & Kaminski, 2005) as a regular assessment. "The students are doing very well on these assessments," Sallie reports. "I can't claim that it's only because of the poetry, but if I can add some joy to their reading instruction, it certainly isn't hurting them." The students are convinced poetry is helping them become better readers, as their comments attest:

"The poems help you learn more words and I think I sound GOOD!"

"My mom says this makes me better at reading."

"They're funny and this helps you increase your reading level."

"My dad said, 'You really use a lot of expression when you read!'"

Conclusion

What Sallie is doing may not be unique, but the fact that she continues to do it in spite of the test-score pressure schools face today is a lesson for us all. Sometimes she gets discouraged with the politics that seem to always surround education. "I've been teaching for 31 years and I've seen it all," she says. "All the criticisms of teachers, all the new ideas for teaching better, all the politicians that get involved, all the acronyms." However, there's one thing Sallie knows for sure: "Tim talked about teaching to their hearts. I know we have to teach to their heads and I will do that, but by adding poetry to my teaching, I can also teach to their hearts."

Reflections

1. How do you incorporate poetry into your classroom? After reading this chapter, did you think of other ways to include poetry?

2. Are your students aware of reasons for reading aloud in life, or do they view reading aloud simply as a part of schoolwork? How could you change their perceptions of oral reading?

3. How might the Lucky Listener's Club work in your own classroom? What adaptations would you have to make?

4. When teachers are asked what their hobbies are, *reading* is usually the first response. When was the last time you read poetry for your own enjoyment? Purchased a book of poems? Recommended a good poem to a friend?

5. How have No Child Left Behind and other governmental mandates for reading instruction affected your teaching?

Fluency as
Response to Intervention
in Waukesha, Wisconsin

The Individuals with Disabilities Education Act (IDEA) is the federal law that secures special education services for children with disabilities from the time they are born until they graduate from high school. With the congressional reauthorization of IDEA in 2004, schools across the nation began looking at learning disabilities through a different lens.

The reauthorized IDEA changed the way children are identified for special services. In the past, a discrepancy between achievement and intellectual ability had to be determined through testing. To prevent over-identification for some students, and "falling through the cracks" for others, a model called Response to Intervention (RTI) replaced the discrepancy formula.

The RTI model calls for tiers of instruction, assessment, and increasingly intense interventions. The first tier consists of research-based instruction in a regular classroom setting accompanied by continual progress monitoring. Students who struggle with the universal curriculum move into the next tier, where they are provided targeted interventions accompanied by progress monitoring. Students who continue to struggle despite receiving research-based interventions are moved to the highest tier, where they are provided special education instruction based on a comprehensive evaluation.

The key to RTI's effectiveness, of course, is high-quality classroom instruction, progress monitoring, and appropriate interventions.

Data Rich, Information Poor

When the RTI model was first proposed as a viable plan for struggling learners, it struck a chord with administrators in the Waukesha, Wisconsin, school district. As leaders in a large district, they saw the full range of learning disabilities.

There was a great deal of discussion about the traditional "discrepancy" and "wait to fail" model of identification. Waukesha leaders realized they needed to be proactive to ensure they were not over-identifying students for learning disabilities. As is true in many districts, data identified a disproportionate number of African American students as EBD (emotional behavior disability). At the same time, they found they had students being identified too late because of the discrepancy model that had been in place for years. To compound matters, the district was also experiencing a dramatic increase in the number of English language learners.

A steering committee was established to lead the RTI initiative. The committee was composed of special education teachers, administrators, school psychologists, and two reading specialists, one of whom was Jennifer Jones.

Prior to establishment of the RTI committee, the district had a solid system in place for monitoring progress. Teachers administered developmentally appropriate assessments in grades K–6, which included letter-sound identification, dictation assessments, ongoing and benchmark running records, cloze passages to assess spelling and comprehension, rhyme awareness, and reading comprehension. Jennifer explains:

> At first, everyone was on board that these assessments, which are administered three times per year, provided the progress monitoring needed and that we needed to work harder to get everyone on the same page with using the data from the assessments to inform instruction. All of that changed when the fine print in IDEA called for "research-based" assessments. This is when all sorts of packaged programs joined the ring for debate and discussion and we, the curriculum folks, became divided from the assessment/data folks. Finally, we put together a very solid monitoring plan.

Assessments included a district-created writing test, the Sunshine Assessment (1996), and the Progress Assessment (1997). All students were to be assessed using multiple measures two or three times a year. In addition, teachers were to use their own assessments to gather data on student progress. It was a good start, but Jennifer realized the new dilemma they faced: We were data rich and information poor. We were not doing the best we could to communicate what we learned from the data," she says. "We are really working now to make the data more useful for teachers. Data that isn't followed by good interventions isn't helpful for students."

RTI Lesson Plan

Jennifer's department began to align and tighten the current system so that RTI would be consistent throughout the district. Through their research, they became convinced a reading workshop approach to intervention made a lot of sense. The goal, Jennifer says, was to "get books in their hands and get them reading. We started moving into a reading workshop model with leveled texts."

All the while, Jennifer continued reading professionally with an eye out for strategies that might work for RTI interventions and that complemented the workshop model. At one point, Richelle Schwechler, a kindergarten teacher, mentioned the parental involvement program called *Fast Start*. (See chapter 4 for more on *Fast Start*.) Jennifer now laughs at her response:

> I said, "Don't show me any canned programs." Shortly after that, I read *The Fluent Reader* (Rasinski, 2003). That book gave me a good understanding that fluency is so much more than reading rate. I also became convinced that we have to teach it. Fluency needed to be a part of our RTI, and I wanted a parent connection. When I realized *Fast Start* was by the same author, I ordered it. When I looked through it, I thought, This is really cool. I went back to the kindergarten teacher and said, "I am so sorry." We started looking at ways to use ideas from *The Fluent Reader* and *Fast Start*.

After adopting these texts, Jennifer and her colleagues began to integrate principles of fluency instruction into reading intervention classes. Students heard, read, and reread short passages that were part of *Fast Start*. Once the passages were mastered, students explored various features of the texts themselves. The short texts in *Fast Start* were perfect for teaching concepts of print. Emergent readers could count the lines in a poem, frame words, locate titles, and point out capital and lowercase letters. Beginning readers could read and reread the short texts to develop fluency.

Teachers and students used magnetic letters for "making and breaking" the words from the *Fast Start* poems. In this exercise, the teacher uses the magnets to make three words with the same rhyme (e.g., i*t, sit, fit; me, be, he; cat, mat, sat*) and reads the words for the child. Next, the teacher makes the words and the student reads them. Finally, the student makes and reads the words. The whole time, the teacher and student are making words and breaking them apart to make them again. "Making and breaking" exemplifies release of responsibility and scaffolding, because the teacher initiates the work and the student takes ownership. As student and teacher work together, the teacher may ask students what they notices about the three words, hoping they will observe that the words have a common vowel or the same ending. The variety of *Fast Start* poems provided easy "making and breaking" words as well as more challenging words as students moved into blends and digraphs.

Richelle and her kindergarten colleague Don LaValle began including exercises from *Fast Start* with their "Book in a Bag" home supplemental intervention program. A couple of nights a week, each student took home a book in a bag that parent and child were to read together. Activities were included in the bag to develop concepts of print, promote listening comprehension, and foster reading enjoyment. As teachers worked on specific reading strategies in class, they chose activities from *Fast Start* that would reinforce that concept.

For example, if students were learning the concept of *word*, teachers put a poem from *Fast Start* into the bag with directions for parents to read the poem and ask their child, "How many words are in the first line of the poem? How about the last line? Which line has more words?" (Padak & Rasinski, 2005, p. 41). They met individual needs by choosing one of three activities listed for the poem that fit each child's needs.

Then, reading aides and teaching assistants in two different kindergarten classrooms began using *Fast Start* with struggling readers. Many of these students couldn't manage independent reading time effectively, so the aides and assistants pulled them aside and provided one-on-one instruction following the program's directions for parents. Often, they expanded on the activities, taking students a step further. This might include, for example, the use of sentence strips for sequencing the *Fast Start* poem, Elkonin boxes for decoding skills, or magnetic letters for making words. Rereading a *Fast Start* poem was also a commonly used strategy for building fluency. Jennifer comments, "So often, we have aides and assistants and we aren't sure how to utilize them effectively. With *Fast Start*, the guess work is gone and the time spent with the aide is time well spent."

After Jennifer's success with *Fast Start*, a group of teachers went to a workshop with Dr. Jean Feldman (drjean.org). Soon teachers throughout the district were using fluency strategies from the workshop with *Fast Start* materials. Dr. Feldman, an early childhood specialist, makes great use of rhyme, song, and movement—perfect contexts for fluency development. Feldman taught teachers to use echo reading, in which teachers read a line and then students repeat the line, and choral reading, where everyone reads together.

Feldman taught the teachers how to use different voices and emotions. For example, she explained how they should teach students to read *Fast Start* poems Papa Bear–style (deep voice), Mama Bear–style (prissy voice), and Baby Bear–style (wee voice). Feldman modeled how teachers and students should read the texts with different emotions, such as sleepy, angry, happy, and sad. In other examples, Feldman had workshop participants put their feet up on their desks, fold their arms over their chests, and read like the "boss," or straddle their chairs and read like cowboys and cowgirls.

In the wake of her district's embracing of Fast Start, Jennifer reflects:

> It was even great for struggling second and third graders. They didn't know the poems. So many kids aren't coming to school with nursery rhymes. They don't hear the rhyming and cadence. These older students also became very engaged in the performance angle when reading the poems. Sometimes I would even take them to read their poem to the librarian, principal, or whomever we might find in the hall. They started to see themselves as readers, and because the *Fast Start* passages were short, it was much easier to get these struggling kids to want to reread. In addition, classroom teachers were collecting formal and informal running records, so very often I would take a quick running record with the *Fast Start* passages—first, on a cold read prior to any teaching, and again after the student had read the poem.

Evidence of Success

Fluency as Response to Intervention is growing in the district. All kindergarten through third-grade teachers are required to take a three-credit graduate course taught by district staff, backed by a local university, and modeled after the work of Marie Clay and Reading Recovery (Clay, 1993). Instruction in fluency strategies has become a component of the district course, and it's paying off.

More kindergarten teachers have indicated they want to use *Fast Start* as a take-home fluency program. A learning disabilities teacher is using it with first- through fourth-grade students. Reading aides say they appreciate the short passages because kids feel successful when they can manage the shorter texts. The principal, Jenny Wimmer of White Rock Elementary, likes having a parent resource for supporting classroom efforts at home. She also likes the fact that anyone can implement the program—classroom teacher, aide, or parent volunteer. As a traveling teacher, Jennifer found *Fast Start* provides research-based best-practice lesson plans that require little preparation, allowing her to meet with students on her tight schedule and have authentic activities readily available.

An exciting side note to the growing interest in *Fast Start* in the district is that Jennifer recently recommended the program to a kindergarten teacher who went on to teach summer school to Hurricane Katrina victims in New Orleans. Jennifer told the teacher *Fast Start* would be perfect because it requires little preparation and few materials, and the students can keep the reading passages.

In addition to teachers, parents are excited about the initiative. One parent wrote a note to Richelle and returned it with her son's Book in a Bag. "Joey read a Dr. Seuss book all by himself!" she wrote. She expressed how proud and excited she was that her son was reading so well. Several parents told Richelle they appreciated the strategies being sent home because it helped them know what to do with their children as readers.

Most importantly, teachers have noticed that students who need reading intervention are more willing to take risks and try to read once they have heard a *Fast Start* poem read. At the end of the first year of the project, 77 percent of kindergarten students (34 of 44) in two participating classrooms were reading at or above the kindergarten exit benchmark for the district. Half of the kindergartners who did not meet the benchmark missed it by only one reading level; they were at guided reading level 3 instead of the district benchmark 4.

Conclusion

As schools use the Response to Intervention model, it is imperative that interventions be carefully chosen and implemented so struggling readers can make the most gains in the least amount of time. The National Reading Panel (2000) identified fluency as one of five instructional factors, supported by empirical research, to be critical to students' overall reading development. Teachers who understand the importance of fluency along with the other four components— vocabulary, comprehension, phonics, and phonemic awareness—are "information rich" and can make Response to Intervention work for students.

Reflections

1. Does your school or district employ a Response to Intervention model? If so, what does the plan include?

2. How do you decide what interventions to provide for struggling readers? To what extent has fluency been identified as an issue for your intervention students?

3. How do you monitor progress of struggling readers?

4. Do you use take-home activities? Please describe them. Could you extend them for classroom use as well?

5. What materials do teacher aides and teacher assistants use to help your students? What challenges do they face? Describe any ideas from this chapter for other instructional activities they could do with students.

Recorded Reading
in Forest Hill, Maryland

Struggling readers are sometimes so caught up in word recognition, or decoding, they forget what "real" reading should sound like. Recorded reading is a way to model and support fluency, build word recognition, and enhance comprehension at the same time. Reading material is recorded in a fluent voice, and the student reads the text while simultaneously hearing the recorded voice of a more fluent reader. The student reads and listens to the passage repeatedly until he or she is able to read it fluently without the assistance of the recording.

Research has shown that seeing a text while simultaneously hearing it can have a profound impact on students' ability to recognize the words in text accurately and fluently (Carbo, 1978, 1981; Rasinski & Hoffman, 2003; Smith & Elley, 1997). It has been found to be especially productive for English language learners. In one study (Koskinen et. al, 1999), ELL students reported practicing almost daily with books and tapes with which they were provided. Most encouraging, the least proficient ELL readers were the ones most likely to practice recorded reading at home.

The third and fourth graders in the intervention class at Forest Lakes Elementary School were quickly losing confidence in their ability to read. Their teachers had tried everything they could think of, with little or no success. The students had been in a structured phonics program—and were still not making it. "Our hearts were breaking," K–5 reading specialist Jennifer Palmer says. "We desperately needed something else." One day, Jennifer found something else—something that finally worked.

Jennifer read Marie Carbo's work recommending "talking books." Carbo (1989) describes a process wherein books and other texts are tape-recorded so the student can read along with a more fluent reader. Carbo also talks about the importance of tailoring instruction to each student's needs. It all made sense to Jennifer, and she started creating tapes immediately. Not long after the project began, Timothy Rasinski spoke at a county in-service meeting. "He validated what we were doing," Jennifer explains. "Now we were really excited to see what results we would get."

Recorded Reading Lesson Plan

Jennifer teaches side by side in the intervention class with special education teacher Lauren Kimmel and classroom teacher Jennifer Vanskiver, so she was very familiar with the students and the problems they were experiencing. She decided to begin recorded reading with students who were furthest behind; they were reading several years below grade level.

The goal was for each student to read along with a tape for 20 minutes every day. During classroom SSR (sustained silent reading) time, two or three students would go to a listening center and read along with tapes. Students would complete three repetitions of the recorded reading and then read it to the teacher.

"Then I started taping and experimenting," Jennifer says. Because the goal was to meet students' needs, the taping had to be individualized. Decisions had to be made—how much to put on a tape, how slow or fast to read, how much new vocabulary would be acceptable, how much background would be needed for comprehension.

Jennifer chose several high-interest, nonfiction books with end-of-first-grade readability. "I chose nonfiction because I didn't want them to think they were reading baby books. They were very interested in nonfiction topics like animals, sports, and natural disasters," she explains. She also downloaded leveled guided-reading stories from the website Reading A to Z (readinga-z.com), which the students could take home for extra practice. Because the school subscribed to the website, there were no copyright issues for the Reading A to Z books. "Remember, this was not a pullout intervention," explains Jennifer. "Since the kids were in the classroom with [non-intervention] kids, we needed to make sure the books were attractive to those kids, too." Once the intervention students were finished with the taped books, other students in the class had the opportunity to use the recorded books, and they often did.

Jennifer cites some specific situations to explain how a plan of action evolved:

> In one case, we gave two kids of the same reading level the same tape. Both of them listened to the 20-minute reading. Andrea did just fine. After three repetitions, she could read the text pretty well. Charles,* on the other hand, was overwhelmed. He has been diagnosed with auditory processing problems. We found if we gave him one third of the book at a time and read more slowly, he was far more successful. Then there were the students with attention deficit disorder. If I taped too slowly for them, I'd lose them. I went back to the students' formal testing records and worked with the special education teacher to decide how to tweak the tapes. After two or three sessions, we had it.

The teachers wanted to build fluency, but they recognized "it wasn't just about smooth and accurate reading, but also about understanding," says Jennifer. For some students, Jennifer had to include information on the tape to build background knowledge. For others, vocabulary instruction was included on the tape.

*All names are pseudonyms.

Creating the tapes became a time-consuming process. Jennifer enlisted the help of other teachers, first the special education teacher and then the homeroom teachers of the students. Principal Linda Chamberlin provided time in the summer for additional taping. The next step was to train PTA volunteers to help make the tapes.

Students listened, read, reread, and ultimately were successful at making meaning through reading. "The students really liked it," Jennifer reports. "For the first time, they sounded fluent. Reading was making sense to them."

Evidence of Success

The first thing the teachers noted was increased confidence. The students began asking for tapes. The teachers often asked, "Which books would you like taped?" Alana brought a chapter book to Jennifer that she had bought at the school's book fair and said, "I really want to read this. I know it's hard. Can you make a tape?" Jennifer confided to us, "The book was not my cup of tea, but I said, 'Oh, yes!' and chose key pieces to record." Jennifer says she reasoned that doing this would provide enough support that "if she wanted to go to other chapters, she could."

As confidence grew, so did reading achievement. The teachers used multiple measures to track progress, including county benchmark tests, the Scholastic Reading Inventory (1999), the Qualitative Reading Inventory (Leslie & Caldwell, 2005), and running records. Alana passed the county benchmark reading test that year. Before recorded reading, She was reading at a first-grade level. She ended the year reading at a beginning third-grade level.

Charles, a student with multiple disabilities, was a non-reader before recorded reading. "We were really worried about him. His mom was really worried about him," Jennifer says. He had received "lots of different interventions." Charles made one year's growth during his first year with recorded reading.

Brent enrolled as a new student in the middle of the year. Jennifer tells his story:

> Brent was a rough kid. He came to us saying, "You can't make me read. I'm not reading. I hate school. I hate my teachers." I told him, "I don't blame you. We just haven't found the best way to teach you yet." I wanted something I thought he'd relate to and so I chose Jack Prelutsky's poem which begins "Homework! Oh, Homework! I hate you, you stink." Of course, he thought it was pretty funny. Over the next several days, we read more poems together from *The New Kid on the Block* (Prelutsky, 1984). He decided with me which ones we would record. Before long, he was reading it back to me. My eyes were getting bigger and bigger, and he was leaning into me for a hug. I said, "Brent, do you know how you sound?"

Brent showed one and a half years' growth during the year he was in the recorded reading program. Jennifer laughs and says, "Here was this biker, skateboarder guy saying, 'Give me another poem."

Not only did the students show progress, but they maintained that progress. When the teachers returned to the books several months later, the students could still read them fluently.

Jennifer reports, "Parents are thrilled. They are seeing the increased confidence we are seeing. They report that their children read more at home, are more interested in books, and want to come to school!"

Conclusion

As of this writing, the recorded reading strategy has been in place at Forest Lakes Elementary School for two years. The teachers see no end to it. While creating tapes can be time-consuming, Jennifer and her co-teacher Lauren see no choice. Their "hearts were breaking" for those students who faced failure day in, and day out. Now those students are reading and succeeding. For the first time they are fluent.

Reflections

1. What does the phrase *reading while listening* mean to you?

2. Describe a dependent reader. Are there different levels of dependence? How can you move a student toward independence?

3. Do you have students for whom nothing seems to work? Talk about what you have tried and the results you got.

4. Fluency will not develop if students merely listen and do not follow along in the text. How can you assure yourself that students are reading when they are listening to tapes?

5. Recording takes time. Brainstorm possible solutions to this time dilemma.

Recorded Books Intervention Record Sheet

Student Name: _____ Date: _____

Text	Level	% Accuracy After Listening Three Times	Rate After Listening Three Times	Comprehension/ Retelling After Listening Three Times

Showcasing Fluency

in Tampa, Florida

The Fluency Masterpiece Gallery is a school program adopted from the art world. Just as artists and photographers showcase their best works or masterpieces at an art opening, students showcase their reading fluency during Fluency Masterpiece Gallery. Parents, relatives, and community members are invited to an evening reception at which students read poems, stories, or scripts they have been writing and or reading in school. It is a gala event with accompanying art displays, simple costumes, and refreshments.

To achieve fluency, the ability to perform at a masterpiece level, students need to practice their performance. This practice is a form of guided and authentic repeated readings, a fluency method that has been shown to be effective in improving students' reading fluency and overall reading proficiency (Rasinski & Hoffman, 2003).　.

The Fluency Masterpiece Gallery

Rylene Stein, principal at the University of South Florida Patel Charter School (USF Patel), had a problem—actually a couple of problems. She was looking for more participation from parents (the same faithful few showed up for every PTA meeting), and she was trying to improve her students' fluency. She hit upon a way that addressed both. Rylene explains:

> We might get six parents to show up at meetings, 12 at the most. We needed to get more parents involved and to be more inclusive. Our population is 87% African American, 1% Asian, 1% Indian, and 8% Hispanic. That diversity was not what we saw at the parent meetings. I asked the staff, "What is it we really want when we have parent meetings?" They said, "We'd like to show off our kids' work." My fine arts background caused me to think, "Galleries!" Rylene explains her vision:

People would come at their leisure, circle, critique, pose questions. Just like artists in a gallery, students would stand back and see how other's react to their work. Then they could jump back in to interact with the audience. Everyone would be invited.

The Masterpiece Gallery Lesson Plan

USF Patel now hosts six masterpiece galleries a year. Each gallery has a different focus, but every year, several galleries are devoted to reading fluency. Two grade levels are showcased at each one, however, everyone is invited, not just the families of the featured students. Dozens of parents, grandparents, aunts and uncles, siblings, and neighbors show up to share in the students' masterpiece work. Guests are given a box lunch. Sometimes the school picks up the cost and sometimes participants are charged an affordable fee, usually $2. The Masterpiece Gallery lasts no more than one hour, an important point for busy families.

There was standing room only at a recent kindergarten and fifth-grade Masterpiece Gallery. The kindergarten Gallery showcased the culmination of a Dr. Seuss unit while the fifth-grade Gallery showcased the products of a unit on peace.

Kindergarten Masterpiece Gallery

Prior to Masterpiece Gallery, the two kindergarten classes had spent three weeks working on reading fluency, compliments of Dr. Seuss. Throughout the unit, teachers Kelly Kleiner and Maria LeFamina read aloud 10 Seuss books. Students were naturally immersed in fluency as they listened with glee to the teachers' reading rate, phrasing, and intonation. Before long, students were chiming in on repeated readings and selecting the books for sustained silent reading.

To develop word automaticity so that the students could actually read the books, Kelly and Maria used activities from the book *I Am Not Going to Read Any Words Today! Learn About Rhyming Words* (Hayward & Goldsmith, 1995). In the mornings, the teachers and children talked about fluency, word families, and rhyming.

In the afternoons, they practiced Readers Theater scripts that Kelly adapted from the Dr. Seuss books. As they practiced fluency, they also learned new vocabulary words. Kelly used terms like *script, performance,* and *director.* She also worked with the children on social skills that would be necessary for a successful Masterpiece Gallery. They learned to stand still while someone else was reading, to be respectful, and to follow along on their script. "They really wanted to read," Kelly says, laughing. "Denae was mad at me. She put her hands on her hips and said indignantly, 'Ms. Kleiner! I only have one line!'" After several days of practice, each student chose which Dr. Seuss book they wanted to showcase for the Gallery.

Now what the children needed was an audience! They made invitations for their parents, relatives, and friends, as well as for university faculty and board members, and then waited impatiently for the evening to arrive.

The kindergarten Masterpiece Gallery began with the Readers Theater script for *The Cat in the Hat* (Seuss, 1957). Kelly had put the text onto chart paper, and one student used a pointer so the audience could follow along on the chart as other students read their scripts. In addition to reading along, parents were given a parent participation sheet. Prior to Masterpiece Gallery, they had been helping their children with sight words at home, so during the performance they were asked to listen for those words and list them on their participation sheet. Children would check their parents' list later. Rylene explains, "Parents are always involved in some way. We are striving to get away from the curriculum fair or art fair format where people just come and passively observe."

In keeping with Readers Theater tradition, students did not wear elaborate costumes. "Keep the focus on reading," is Kelly's advice to others. "We don't want anything to take away from their performance." The Cat in the Hat simply wore a black shirt and pants and Maria offered up a red scarf. Halfway through the performance, the cast discovered that one of the main characters, Mother, was not there. The Cat in the Hat took off her red scarf, picked up the mother's script, and proclaimed, to the delight of the audience, "Oh, I'll just do it," and proceeded to read two parts.

Refreshments for the evening? Green eggs and ham, of course!

Fifth-Grade Masterpiece Gallery

That same evening, fifth-grade students shared their Masterpiece Gallery based on a holiday unit on peace. Teachers Julie Moors and Autumn Laidler explained that many of their students do not celebrate traditional holidays, so they designed a unit on peace to correspond with Veterans Day. The teachers used ideas from "Peace Poems and Picasso Doves: Literature, Art, Technology, and Poetry" from readwritethink.org, a website supported by the International Reading Association and the National Council of Teachers of English.

The teachers modeled fluency throughout the unit as they read aloud stories and poems from books such as *An Angel for Solomon Singer* (Rylant, 1996) and *Smoky Night* (Bunting, 1999). Literacy activities rich with fluency wove their way through the unit. Students wrote and read acrostic peace poems. Students and teachers collaborated in grading the poems with a rubric (see page 101). Students wrote essays on "What Peace Means to Me," and read them orally in class. They brainstormed lists of words beginning with *p* that represent peace.

The teachers integrated art into the unit (certainly appropriate for a Gallery!) as they connected to Picasso's famous peace dove painting. Students made peace pinwheels and origami cranes to serve as centerpieces for tables at Masterpiece Gallery.

As Masterpiece Gallery drew near, students had the choice to work independently or collaborate with others to create peace displays that included an original piece of artwork with a dove incorporated, a personal poem about peace, and an origami crane from their reading of *Sadako and the Thousand Paper Cranes* (Coerr, 2005). On the evening of the Gallery, the walls of the cafeteria were covered with colorful posters. Julie comments, "The kids were thrilled when they saw it all set up. It all came together. It was impressive!"

Fluency was front and center as the students shared their peace projects. The presentations ranged from describing an experience in nature, to what peace means to them personally, to how they see or want to see peace in the world. One student's poem focused on a description of the peaceful sound of a running river and had an art piece to match. Another student described a peaceful day with family sharing food, laughs, and gifts. Another memorable peace poem spoke of peace in the student's country of origin, a Middle Eastern country, and why peace is necessary there.

When the program began, the teachers requested that applause be held till the end, but members of the audience could not comply with the request. Each student received a strong round of applause after his or her reading. Autumn reflects, "The students read their poems with such strength and passion. It was a very moving experience, especially at a time of holidays and yet uncertainty in the world."

Evidence of Success

Principal

Rylene calls the Fluency Masterpiece Gallery a "principal's dream." She shared that the Galleries "have really brought in the crowds." Parents feel more connected to the school. "They used to say, 'You never communicate.' I never hear that anymore," she says with satisfaction.

> Parents have a more intimate involvement with their own child and they see the results of what is happening in the whole school. Parents are so proud. We are showcasing their child. Attendance has increased because the word is out that you get to see the kids, not just papers hanging on the walls.

Most gratifying, however, is the sense of accomplishment and pride Rylene observes in the students. "Students actually have an opportunity to make their learning real," she states. She can tell story after story of individual children who have surprised everyone with their marvelous presentations. "Each student's work is a masterpiece," Rylene brags.

Teachers

USF Patel Charter School teachers are excited about the learning they know is spurred by Masterpiece Gallery. Autumn calls Masterpiece Gallery the "hook" to get students practicing fluency. "Kids get really excited. Just using the word *masterpiece,* kids think, 'Wow!' Just the term invites quality work." Julie adds, "You know how much they are learning, but when they get up and present, it blows you away." The teachers believe parent turnout is so high because students are excited about sharing their work. "They talk about it for weeks before the parents actually receive an invitation," Kelly says.

Not only is parent attendance high for Masterpiece Gallery, but student attendance in school increases for Masterpiece Gallery draws near. The teachers comment that students want to be in school so they can prepare. In fact, some students are disappointed when they are ill or have doctor appointments. They tell their teachers, "Wait till I get back!" In fact, Autumn says laughing, "If a child had to go to the bathroom, he would say, 'Don't start yet!' as he dashed out the door."

The excitement of Masterpiece Gallery carries into everyday reading. Kelly says, "On a regular basis they are saying, 'Please, please, please can we read?'" Julie chimes in, "That's happening in fifth grade, too. They *want* to share what they're writing even apart from Masterpiece Gallery."

Julie reflects on bringing the grades together. "It was nice to pair kindergarten with fifth grade. Parents got to see the beginning point and ending point of our school—what the works looks like at kindergarten and what it looks like at fifth grade."

Parents

The parents' attendance is evidence of success in and of itself. In addition, they frequently comment about the benefits of Masterpiece Gallery. "We never did this kind of thing before," one mother comments. "I'm so glad my child has a chance to do this!"

The father of a particularly quiet, struggling reader couldn't believe his son had written such an insightful poem. "I was so proud of the way he read it in front of a crowd on Masterpiece night," he says. He explains that the peace unit had really engaged his son. "It made me feel so proud to see him express himself both in writing and art!"

The parent of a fifth grader new to the school told Julie, "It was hard deciding whether to send Kyla to a charter school. The night I came to Masterpiece Gallery, I knew I did the right thing." She continued,

> I really know my daughter is being challenged to think critically about things she is learning. Not only is she reading better, she is also making connections to the world around her. In her other school, the kids were taught so much so quickly, and they often barely scratched the surface.

Students

Although the principal's, teachers', and parents' testimonials are important, students' comments are the real test. Here's what some kindergartners had to say:

Hannah: I like Readers Theater because my mom came to school to watch me.

Alicia: I like acting in plays because maybe I will be on TV one day.

Danae: It made my brain think about school all the time because I wanted to be the Cat!

Julie reports about a student's reaction,

One student who enjoys art was totally blown away by the origami cranes and the story of Sadako and her efforts to promote peace in the world. It made her realize that children *can* and *do* make a difference in the world. She said that usually when people talk about peace, they only focus on past and current wars, and the efforts of the military. She thought it was powerful to think of peace in our everyday world, and how each of us could make a difference, no matter how small the contribution. She went on to make cranes for all her family members who attended a family reunion, and told them the story of Sadako. How cool!

Conclusion

USF Patel Charter School no longer struggles for parent involvement. Parents are now getting involved in a way that is meaningful to them and to their children. Every student's work is a Masterpiece, and the celebrations that surround their work have had a great impact. Rylene and her teachers continually ask the students, "What are you here for?" They respond with enthusiasm, "A great day of learning!" Having real work for a real audience has made the difference.

Reflections

1. What is your goal for parent events or meetings?

2. How could you showcase students' fluency progress?

3. Does your school have a way for parents to participate in student work?

4. How many parents attend PTA meetings at your school? Could some meetings be used for a Fluency Masterpiece Gallery?

5. Does your school have a curriculum fair or art show where parents are passive observers of student work? If so, could it be restructured so that students and parents participate in celebrating student work?

Grade 5 Rubric for Student-Created Peace Poetry

Student Name: _____

Poem Title: _____

Self-evaluate your poem by writing your **initials** in the box that best represents your work. Give **examples** to show why you deserve that score. Total your **points** at the bottom of the page.

Criteria	5	4	3	2	1
Content and Ideas	This poem shares **powerful** ideas related to the peace theme. Example(s):	This poem shares **strong** ideas related to the peace theme. Example(s):	This poem shares **good** ideas related to the peace theme. Example(s):	This poem shares **adequate** ideas related to the peace theme. Example(s):	This poem shares **weak** ideas related to the peace theme. Example(s):
Voice	This peace poem creates a **powerful** reaction in the reader or listener. Example(s):	This peace poem creates a **strong** reaction in the reader or listener. Example(s):	This peace poem **sometimes** creates a reaction in the reader or listener. Example(s):	This peace poem creates a **slight** reaction in the reader or listener. Example(s):	This peace poem **does not** create a reaction in the reader or listener. Example(s):
Word Choice Adjectives Action Verbs Similes Metaphors Alliteration	This peace poem uses **powerful, engaging,** and **precise** words. Example(s):	This peace poem uses **strong** and **precise** words. Example(s):	This peace poem uses **ordinary** words. Example(s):	This peace poem uses **adequate** and **nonspecific** words. Example(s):	This peace poem uses **lifeless** words. Example(s):
Organization	This poem **flows** and is **organized** to make a **powerful** impact on the reader or listener Example(s):	This poem **flows** and is **organized** to make a **strong** impact on the reader or listener. Example(s):	This poem is **organized** but **does not flow or make a strong impact** on the reader or listener. Example(s):	This poem is **not organized** to make an impact on the reader or listener. Example(s):	This poem **confuses** the reader or listener. Example(s):

Student's Points: _____   Teacher's Points: _____   Total Points: _____

Finding an Answer to
Summer School Attitude in Mayfield, Ohio

Every summer, some students lose as much as a full grade level in reading skills. Other students, however, maintain or even gain skills over the summer. What makes the difference? Summer reading! (McGill-Franzen & Allington, 2005; Mraz & Rasinski, 2007). Yet, which children are least likely to read in the summer? Those who need it most. After months or even years of failure, struggling readers welcome the summer, during which there is no reading class, no reading teacher, and no school library.

Richard Allington and Anne McGill-Franzen (2003) explain summer reading loss in a way that grabs one's attention:

> If schools had some children read virtually nothing during the first three months of school, then the negative effect on reading development would be observable. If some children read virtually nothing during June, July, and August, then we might also expect a negative impact on reading development (pages. 71–72).

Many children who struggle with reading are assigned to summer school, where they get a hefty dose of skills instruction but little time for extended reading. More often than not, these same children continue to struggle during the regular school year.

Summer Readers Theater is an alternative to the traditional summer school model. Rather than skill drills, the focus is on developing fluency through repeated reading of engaging plays, poems, and songs.

A New Image for Summer School

Students were mad, parents were frustrated, and teachers were bored. Every year, the *summer school attitude* played out in Mayfield, Ohio, just as it was playing out in districts across the country. Children longed to ride bikes rather than yellow buses; parents threatened and cajoled their children every morning; and teachers taught the same lessons that did not work during the school year with these children. To add insult to injury, it was a rare child who showed much improvement when the new school year began.

The district analyzed midyear K–5 achievement data for all students who attended *summer school*. No one was really surprised at the results. Summer school was not working. There were a number of reasons. First, the summer school attitude. Traditionally, summer school has been synonymous with failure. Teachers and parents threaten children that if they do not work hard during the year, they will have to attend the dreaded summer school.

Second, while students needed all the skills that were being taught, the curriculum was too broad for the amount of time teachers had to work with students. In Mayfield, summer school started as soon as the school year ended and it lasted four weeks. The gap between the end of summer school and the beginning of the new school year allowed many students to lose any progress they might have made. Summer school wasn't really doing anything well.

After puzzling over the dilemma, Lou Kindervater, the summer school principal, threw out an idea to Gay Fawcett, district curriculum director, and Tammi Bender, district literacy specialist. Why not move summer school to the last few weeks of the summer and make Readers Theater the focus? By the time August rolls around most students are beginning to get excited about returning to school, and the later time frame could help students hang onto their gains because of the minimal instructional gap. A program called Summer Readers Theater would sound more appealing than summer school, so students would be more agreeable to attending. Most importantly, Readers Theater would eliminate the overloaded curriculum and focus instruction on fluency, a skill with a lot of leverage.

Immediately, Lou, Gay, and Tammi began planning the much-needed summer school change. They threw out the old skills-based curriculum and began collecting Readers Theater scripts and poems. They downloaded some from the Internet for free and they purchased some. They bought a copy of *The Fluent Reader* (Rasinski, 2003) and a *Fluency First!* kit (Rasinski & Padak, 2005b) for each summer school teacher.

Tammi provided intensive teacher training, and teachers gained a new appreciation for the role of fluency in learning to read. They understood the importance of accuracy, automaticity, and intonation, and they learned new strategies to teach fluency. Tammi also trained the teachers to assess fluency using 3-Minute Reading Assessments (Rasinski & Padak, 2004, 2005a).

Lou worked with the teachers to establish expectations for a positive climate. He shared his view of their role as "coaches" and underscored the importance of modeling fluency. He suggested they sit on the floor with students and have fun with Readers Theater. He asked the secretary to answer the phone by saying, "Hello. This is Mayfield Readers Theater." Lou's leadership initiatives resulted in a feeling of community and common purpose among students, parents, and teachers.

Each elementary school notified parents of the upcoming summer school change through their school newsletter. The district purchased T-shirts for each enrolled child with a Summer Readers Theater logo encircling a picture of children. Each grade received a different color T-shirt and matching pocket folders to hold their Readers Theater scripts.

Summer Readers Theater Begins

On the first day, there was an altercation among three students on the playground. Lou describes what happened:

> I never have discipline problems with summer school, so I was surprised. I took them to the office and started talking to them about the expectations. I said, "The rules in summer school are the same as the rules during regular school." One little guy— the instigator, a tough little kid— interrupted me. He said, "I don't go to summer school! I'm at Readers Theater." It changed my whole demeanor. I said, "You're right." It changed me. That kid was so proud to be at Readers Theater rather than in summer school.

Summer Readers Theater Lesson Plan

Summer Readers Theater instruction was comprised of explicit fluency instruction and Readers Theater script practice. Teachers incorporated writing by having students create scripts. Older students wrote their own scripts with teacher guidance, and younger students dictated scripts that the teachers wrote on chart paper. Favorite scripts included familiar tales such as "The Three Little Pigs," "The Three Billy Goats Gruff," and "The Little Red Hen." Students frequently asked if they could write a script after a teacher shared a story during read-aloud. Some of their favorites were *The Enormous Turnip* (Parkinson, 1986), *Click, Clack, Moo* (Cronin, 2000), and *Where the Wild Things Are* (Sendak, 1964).

Every Friday, each class performed their scripts on the auditorium stage, complete with their T-shirts, matching folders, and microphone. The performances were scheduled so that parents could come during their lunch breaks. Some parents didn't miss a single performance. Also in attendance were grandparents, siblings, and district staff who worked through the summer.

Evidence of Success

Lou reflects, "There's always been something about the way we do oral reading as teachers. I don't know . . . " his voice trailed off. "But this is so right! The kids were so comfortable. The security they had—I'd never seen that in a summer program before. We could feel it."

Students

Some of the best reports of progress came the following fall from the students themselves. One of Tammi's responsibilities as district literacy specialist was to help teachers in the regular classroom administer 3-Minute Reading Assessments. On more than one occasion, a student expressed delight as they began the assessment. Amanda exclaimed, "I know how to do this! I did this in Summer Readers Theater. Before that, I didn't do so well with reading, but now I do."

Tammi tells about another student she tested:

> It was the first day of school, and I was doing the 3-Minute with all the sixth graders. One boy was a special education student who had gone to Summer Readers Theater. As I started telling him what we were going to do, he interrupted me. He said, "Oh, you're giving me this. I know exactly how to do this. I went to Readers Theater this summer." He was so pumped up. He was so proud. He read beautifully. In fact, his reading rate was the highest in the class, and his comprehension too was very high.

In the fall, regular classroom teachers reported that the Summer Readers Theater students were asking to "do things." The teachers told Lou that the students wanted to work in groups, to do plays, to do poetry. "They were looking up plays," Lou says, laughing.

Parents

Parents completed a survey that showed their satisfaction with the program (see page 106). But comments on the survey provided information that a simple circling of responses could not. Here are just a few responses:

> "Jacob loved the fact that he performed songs in front of the whole school the first week!"

> "He also went to summer camp, and he liked summer school better. Wow!"

> "I think it's wonderful that Allison couldn't wait to go to school! Thank you for this program!"

> "Jessica said she never wanted it to end. It's so nice to see how proud the children are of their week's work at Readers Theater. A lot of smiles on kids' faces."

> "We don't make reading aloud to us a normal practice. Now we will

change that."

Months after Summer Readers Theater ended, one of the teachers was in the

Summer Readers Theater Parent Survey Results

1. My child was initially happy about coming to Summer Readers Theater.

Year	Yes	No	Not sure
2006	62%	27%	11%
2005	62%	20%	18%

2. As Summer Readers Theater progressed, my child:

Year	Enjoyed it more	Enjoyed it less	Not sure
2006	89%	3%	3%
2005	90%	1%	7%

3. I believe the late-summer dates for Summer Readers Theater will help my child to be better prepared for the new school year.

Year	Yes	No	Not sure
2006	92%	2%	6%
2005	92%	3%	5%

4. During Summer Readers Theater, my child's reading:

Year	Improved	Declined	Stayed about the same	Not sure
2006	58%		36%	2%
2005	67%		18%	15%

supermarket when she heard someone calling her name from the other end of the aisle. She turned to see a parent pushing her cart as fast as it could go so she could catch up before the teacher rounded the corner. "I just wanted to tell you how much I appreciated Summer Readers Theater!" she said. "It was such a great experience for Joey. I am so thankful. His reading has improved so much and he really loved coming."

Teachers

At the end of the first Summer Readers Theater, teachers begged to have the *Fluency First!* kits to use in their own classrooms during the school year. The answer, of course, was *yes*! They took what they had learned about fluency instruction into their own classrooms and began doing Readers Theater on a regular basis with all students. Word got around, and one teacher, Lynne Spector, was asked to have her students do a Readers Theater for a board of education meeting.

Another teacher, Jenifer Wexler, enjoyed teaching Summer Readers Theater so much she decided to write a grant to purchase materials to do Readers Theater with her preschool students, the majority of whom were children with special needs. (See Chapter 1.) What her students accomplished was amazing.

Kelly Sannelli, a third-grade teacher, reflects on the program:

> I think the most amazing thing about Summer Readers Theater is how the students' confidence grows. I have had many students in Readers Theater that I taught during the school year, and I was able to see a different, confident side of them in the summer that I wish I had been able to pull out of them during the school year. For the most part, the children who come to Summer Readers Theater don't feel confident about themselves as readers, but after all the rereading and practice, they are reading with great pacing and expression without even worrying about making mistakes—a huge step for a lot of the kids. I really do think that this confidence transfers into all of their reading. In the fall, when I do my first Readers Theater with my class, I have found a couple of students will pipe up and say that they are good at it or they like it because they did it in the summer.

One unexpected result of the program was that Summer Readers Theater provided the context for some teachers to take on a teacher-leadership role. When Tammi Bender left the position of literacy specialist to become a principal, Lou says he worried:

> I thought we were going to struggle without Tammi. I invited some of the teachers to take on the role of training and mentoring teachers for the second year of Summer Readers Theater. They stepped right up and did an incredible job. They were so committed to the program and wanted to see it continue being successful. They also provided leadership in their own buildings to get more teachers using Readers Theater throughout the year.

Summer Readers Theater Grows

It didn't take long for summer school's new image to take hold. During the second year, parents began calling early to request a spot for their children. One parent said, "We have heard so many good things about it. Kids are excited about performing." Another parent told his child's teacher, "He enjoyed it last year and he wants to return."

A third-grade teacher told Gay she wasn't sure how to handle the Summer Readers Theater conversation taking place among her students. When one struggling reader received an invitation to attend Summer Readers Theater, other students began asking their teacher if they could go also. "I've never had students want to go to summer school before!" she says with a laugh.

Parents from neighboring districts called to ask if their children could attend. When

Lou asked how they heard about Mayfield's Summer Readers Theater, they told him it was being discussed at the baseball field and at the pool. Lou says, "They were so disappointed when I told them there was no room for students outside our district. They said, 'Our district doesn't do anything like this.'" Lou reflects, "Summer Readers Theater has really created a good image for Mayfield."

Enrollment in Summer Readers Theater increased the second year, so that an additional teacher had to be hired. There was such a "flooding of parents" that the Friday performances had to be divided into two sessions. "This is getting around just by word of mouth," Lou reports. "Next year, I expect to need even more teachers."

During the second year, Lou added a new dimension to Summer Readers Theater that provided some good insight for teachers, students, and parents. After some Friday performances, students were dismissed early so that parents could stay and talk with the teachers. Parents were full of questions:

✳ What exactly is fluency?

✳ Why are you doing this?

✳ Why are students not memorizing scripts?

✳ Why aren't they doing more math?

✳ Why don't you call the teachers *directors* like in real-life plays?

Lou and the teachers relished the opportunity to talk about the concept of fluency and its importance in learning to read. They explained that in Readers Theater students don't memorize lines and wear costumes, because the purpose is to improve their reading skills. This also gave them an opportunity to speak about the value of repeated readings.

Lou explained to parents that teachers were viewed more like drama *coaches* than *directors*, and he shared his philosophy of teacher modeling and support. He and the teachers reinforced the importance of reading in math. They told the parents:

> Reading and writing are essential math skills. There's more reading in math than there was when you and I were in school. Students now have to explain their answers—write about how they solved a problem. Improving their reading will also improve their math. We can't separate reading and math.

The students also had a few question-and-answer sessions. Interestingly, the questions they asked were similar to those of their parents.

✳ Why did you decide to do it this way?

✳ Why don't we use props?

* Can I wear a costume?

* Will this make me a better reader?

Again, Lou and the teachers stressed the goal of improved reading and explained the concept of fluency in a way that even the kindergartners could understand.

Another important improvement to Summer Readers Theater in the second year was the addition of content area scripts, which both students and teachers enjoyed immensely. They chose scripts dealing with math, social studies, and science. There was also more work with poetry and more script writing by students.

Conclusion

The *summer school attitude* is gone in Mayfield, Ohio. Students are no longer mad, parents are no longer frustrated, and teachers are excited, not bored. And best of all, students are becoming successful, fluent readers in Summer Readers Theater.

Reflections

1. Are you familiar with your district's summer school curriculum? How would you describe it?

2. Is your district's summer school effective in improving students' reading achievement? How do you know?

3. Is your district's summer school effective in improving students' attitude toward reading? How do you know?

4. How do students and parents in your district feel about summer school?

5. How is fluency addressed in your summer school program?

6. How can summer school staff work with regular classroom teachers to assure continuity between programs?

Readers Theater Script:

The Grasshopper and the Ants

Source: loiswalker.com

This choral speaking version of " The Grasshopper and the Ants" includes a variety of speaker experiences. As in most choral speaking, CHORUS SPEAKERS speak in unison together. But, in an effort to bring needed variety of sound and a composer's touch to the choral expression of this piece, you may find that:

SOLO SPEAKERS speak special lines.

ALL BOYS and/or ALL GIRLS speak in unison together.

SPECIAL QUARTETS speak in unison together.

CHARACTER SPEAKERS (Grasshopper and Ants) speak character lines.

Chorus: There once was a grasshopper

Solo Speaker 1: Who was in a party mood

Chorus: She sang away the summer days
                     And ate up all her food!

Grasshopper: Yo-hoo, that's me!
                     It's true, it's true
                     I ate up all my food!

Chorus: Hey grasshopper Gal!

Hate to burst your bubble

There's a moral to this tale

You're headed straight for trouble!

Girls' Chorus: When winter came she realized

She'd made a big mistake

She hadn't saved a thing to eat

And how her tummy ached

Grasshopper: I haven't saved a thing to eat

And now my tummy aches!

Chorus: Hey grasshopper Gal!

Hate to burst your bubble

There's a moral to this tale

YOU'RE headed straight for trouble!

Boys' Chorus: The ants who lived next door to her

Had planned ahead, in fact

Had worked throughout the summer heat

To store up food out back

Ant Quartet: Did you ever, did you ever

Meet a group of ants so clever?

Chorus: Hey grasshopper Gal!

Hate to burst your bubble

There's a moral to this tale

YOU'RE headed straight for trouble!

Girls' Quartet: And when our dear grasshopper

Came begging for some bread

Boys' Quartet: The ants just shook their heads and said

Ant Quartet: "You're going to end up dead!!"

Chorus: Hey grasshopper Gal!

Hate to burst your bubble

There's a moral to this tale

YOU'RE headed straight for trouble!

Grasshopper: O.K., O.K., I've heard enough!

So what's the moral? Tell me please!

Solo Speaker 2:   I bet the moral's full of DON'TS!

Solo Speaker 3:   Don't sing away the summer?

Solo Speaker 4:   Don't party 'til you're fed?

Solo Speaker 5:   Don't waste your days just having fun?

Solo Speaker 6:   Don't lounge around in bed?

Chorus: NO!

Solo Speaker 7:   The moral of this story is:

Chorus: It's smart to plan ahead!

List of Categories

Professional works that focus on several aspects of fluency

Assessing fluency

Comprehension and fluency

Prosody—Reading with expression

Prosody—Readers Theater

Prosody—Singing and poetry-based approaches to fluency

Prosody—Fluency and English language learners

Automaticity—Reading rate

Automaticity—Repeated reading

Automaticity—Dyad and paired reading

Accuracy—Word study and phonics

Accuracy—Oral reading miscues

Various approaches to promote fluency

Specific programs to promote fluency

General resources on reading instruction

Edited Books on Fluency

Rasinski, T. V. (Ed.) (2009). *Essential readings on fluency.* Newark, DE: International Reading Association.

Rasinski, T.V., Blachowicz, C., & Lems, K. (Eds.). (2006). *Fluency instruction: Research-based best practices.* New York: Guilford.

Samuels, S. J., & Farstrup, A. E. (Eds.). (2006). *What research has to say about fluency instruction.* Newark, DE: International Reading Association.

Professional Works That Focus on Several Aspects of Fluency

Allington, R. L. (1983). Fluency: The neglected goal of the reading program. *The Reading Teacher, 36,* 556–561.

Allington, R. L. (2006). Fluency: Still waiting after all these years. In S. J. Samuels & A. E. Farstrup (Eds.), *What research has to say about fluency instruction* (pp. 94–105). Newark, DE: International Reading Association.

Allington, R. L. (2008). *What really matters in fluency.* Boston: Allyn & Bacon.

Ash, G. E., & Kuhn, M. R. (2006). Meaningful oral and silent reading in the elementary and middle school classroom: Breaking the round robin reading addiction. In T. Rasinski, C. Blachowicz, & K. Lems (Eds.), *Fluency instruction: Research-based best practices* (pp. 155–172). New York: Guilford Press.

Chard, D. J., Vaughn, S., & Tyler, B. (2002). A synthesis of research on effective interventions for building reading fluency with elementary students with learning disabilities. *Journal of Learning Disabilities, 35,* 386–406.

Daane, M. C., Campbell, J. R., Grigg, W. S., Goodman, M. J., & Oranje, A. (2005). *Fourth-grade students reading aloud: NAEP 2002 special study of oral reading.* Washington, DC: U.S. Department of Education, Institute of Education Sciences.

Fuchs, L. S., Fuchs, D., Hosp, M. K., & Jenkins, J. R. (2001). Oral reading fluency as an indicator of reading competence: A theoretical, empirical, and historical analysis. *Scientific Studies of Reading, 5,* 239–256.

Griffith, L. W., & Rasinski, T. V. (2004). A focus on fluency: How one teacher incorporated fluency with her reading curriculum. *The Reading Teacher, 58,* 126–137.

Hoffman, J. V., & Segel, K. (1983, May). *Oral reading instruction: A century of controversy (1880–1980).* Paper presented at the annual meeting of the International Reading Association, Anaheim, CA. (ERIC Document Reproduction Service No. ED239237).

Hyatt, A. V. (1943). *The place of oral reading in the school program: Its history and development from 1880–1941.* New York: Teachers College Press.

Johns, J., & Berglund, R. (2002). *Fluency: Questions, answers, evidence-based strategies.* Dubuque, IA: Kendall Hunt.

Kame'enui, E. J., & Simmons, D. C. (2001a). Introduction to this special issue: The DNA of reading fluency. *Scientific Studies of Reading, 5,* 203–210.

Kame'enui, E. J., & Simmons, D. C. (Eds.). (2001b). The role of fluency in reading competence, assessment, and instruction: Fluency at the intersection of accuracy and speed [Special issue]. *Scientific Studies of Reading, 5*(3).

Keillor, G. (2004). For the week of October 18, 2004. *The Writer's Almanac.* Retrieved April 22, 2007, from http://writersalmanac.publicradio.org/programs/2004/10/18/index.html.

Kuhn, M. R., Schwanenflugel, P. J., Morris, R. D., Morrow, L. M., Woo, D. G., Meisinger, E. B., Stahl, S. A. (2006). Teaching children to become fluent and automatic readers. *Journal of Literacy Research, 38,* 357–387.

Kuhn, M. R., & Stahl, S. A. (2000). *Fluency: A review of developmental and remedial practices.* (CIERA Rep. No. 2-008). Ann Arbor, MI: Center for the Improvement of Early Reading Achievement.

Kuhn, M. R., & Stahl, S. A. (2004). Fluency: A review of developmental and remedial practices. In R. B. Ruddell & N. J. Unrau (Eds.), *Theoretical models and processes of reading* (5th ed., pp. 412-453). Newark, DE: International Reading Association.

Liben, D. (2008). *The unique role fluency plays in adolescent literacy programs.* Unpublished manuscript.

Maro, N. (2001). Reading to improve fluency. *Illinois Reading Council Journal, 29*(3), 10–18.

Pinnell, G. S., Pikulski, J. J., Wixson, K. K., Campbell, J. R., Gough, P. B., & Beatty, A. S. (1995). *Listening to children read aloud.* Washington, DC: U.S. Department of Education, Office of Educational Research and Improvement.

Rasinski, T. V. (1985). *A study of factors involved in reader-text interactions that contribute to fluency in reading.* Unpublished doctoral dissertation, Ohio State University, Columbus.

Rasinski, T. V. (1989). Fluency for everyone: Incorporating fluency in the classroom. *The Reading Teacher, 42,* 690–693.

Rasinski, T. V. (1990c). *The effects of cued phrase boundaries in texts.* Bloomington, IN: ERIC Clearinghouse on Reading and Communication Skills. (ERIC Document Reproduction Service No. ED313689).

Rasinski, T. V. (2004b). Creating fluent readers. *Educational Leadership, 61*(6), 46–51.

Rasinski, T. V. (2006). Reading fluency instruction: Moving beyond accuracy, automaticity, and prosody. *The Reading Teacher, 59,* 704–706.

Rasinski, T. V. (2007). Teaching reading fluency artfully: A professional and personal journey. In R. Fink & S. J. Samuels (Eds.), *Inspiring reading success: Interest and motivation in an age of high-stakes testing* (pp. 117–140). Newark, DE: International Reading Association.

Rasinski, T. V. (2010). *The fluent reader: Oral reading strategies for building word recognition, fluency, and comprehension* (2nd ed.). New York: Scholastic.

Rasinski, T. V., & Hoffman, J. V. (2003). Theory and research into practice: Oral reading in the school literacy curriculum. *Reading Research Quarterly, 38,* 510–522.

Rasinski, T. V., & Padak, N. D. (2005a).Fluency beyond the primary grades: Helping adolescent readers. *Voices from the Middle, 13*(1), 34–41.

Rasinski, T. V., & Padak, N. D. (2008). *From phonics to fluency: Effective teaching of decoding and reading fluency in the elementary school* (2nd ed.). New York: Addison, Wesley, Longman.

Rasinski, T. V., Padak, N. D., Linek, W. L., & Sturtevant, E. (1994). Effects of fluency development on urban second-grade readers. *Journal of Educational Research, 87,* 158–165.

Rasinski, T. V., Padak, N. D., McKeon, C. A., Wilfong, L. G., Friedauer, J. A., & Heim, P. (2005). Is reading fluency a key for successful high school reading? *Journal of Adolescent and Adult Literacy, 49,* 22–27.

Rasinski, T. V., Rikli, A., & Johnston, S. (2009). Reading fluency: More than automaticity? More than a concern for the primary grades? *Literacy Research and Instruction, 48,* 350–361.

Rasinski, T. V., & Zutell, J. B. (1996). Is fluency yet a goal of the reading curriculum? In E. G. Sturtevant & W. M. Linek (Eds.), *Growing literacy* (18th Yearbook of the College Reading Association, pp. 237–246). Harrisonburg, VA: College Reading Association.

Reutzel, D. R. (2006). "Hey, teacher, when you say 'fluency,' what do you mean?": Developing fluency in elementary classrooms. In T. V. Rasinski, C. Blachowicz, & K. Lems (Eds.), *Fluency instruction: Research-based best practices* (pp. 62–85). New York: Guilford.

Reutzel, D.R., Hollingsworth, P. M., & Eldredge, J. L. (1994). Oral reading instruction: The impact on student reading development. *Reading Research Quarterly, 29,* 40–62.

Samuels, S. J. (2002). Reading fluency: Its development and assessment. In A. Farstrup & S. J. Samuels (Eds.), *What research has to say about reading instruction* (3rd ed., pp. 166–183). Newark, DE: International Reading Association.

Schreiber, P. A. (1980). On the acquisition of reading fluency. *Journal of Reading Behavior, 12,* 177–186.

Stahl, S. A. (2004). What do we know about fluency? Findings of the National Reading Panel. In P. McCardle & V. Chhabra (Eds.), *The voice of evidence in reading research* (pp. 187–211). Baltimore, MD: Brookes.

Stahl, S. A., & Heubach, K. (2005). Fluency-oriented reading instruction. *Journal of Literacy Research, 37*(1), 25–60.

Stahl, S. A., Heubach, K., & Cramond, B. (1997). *Fluency-oriented reading instruction* (Reading Research Rep. No. 79). Athens, GA, and College Park, MD: National Reading Research Center.

Stahl, S. A., & Kuhn, M. R. (2002). Making it sound like language: Developing fluency. *The Reading Teacher, 55,* 582–584.

Stanovich, K. E. (1980). Toward an interactive-compensatory model of individual differences in the development of reading fluency. *Reading Research Quarterly, 16,* 32–71.

Strecker, S., Roser, N., & Martinez, N. (1998). Toward an understanding of oral reading fluency. In T. Shanahan & F. Rodriguez-Brown (Eds.), *47th yearbook of the National Reading Conference* (pp. 295–310). Chicago: National Reading Conference.

Walker, B. J., Mokhtari, K., & Sargent, S. (2006). Reading fluency: More than fast and accurate reading. In T. Rasinski, C. Blachowicz, & K. Lems (Eds.), *Fluency instruction: Research-based best practices* (pp. 86–105). New York: Guilford Press.

Worthy, J., & Broaddus, K. (2002). Fluency beyond the primary grades: From group performance to silent, independent reading. *The Reading Teacher, 55*, 334–343.

Zutell, J., Donelson, R., Bevans, J., & Todt, P. (2006). Building a focus on oral reading fluency into individual instruction for struggling readers. In T. V. Rasinski, C. Blachowicz, & K. Lems (Eds.), *Fluency instruction: Research-based best practices* (pp. 265–278). New York: Guilford.

Zutell, J., & Rasinski, T. V. (1991). Training teachers to attend to their students' oral reading fluency. *Theory Into Practice, 30*(3), 211–217.

Assessing Fluency

Beaver, J. (1999). *Developmental reading assessment.* New York: Scott Foresman.

Blachowicz, C. Z., Sullivan, D. M., & Cieply, C. (2001). Fluency snapshots: A quick screening tool for your classroom. *Reading Psychology, 22*, 95–109.

Deno, S. L. (1985). Curriculum-based measurement: The emerging alternative. *Exceptional Children, 52*, 219–232.

Deno, S. L., Mirkin, P. K., & Chiang, B. (1982). Identifying valid measures of reading. *Exceptional Children, 49*, 36–45.

Good, R. H., III, & Kaminski, R. (2005). DIBELS: *Dynamic indicators or basic early literacy skills* (6th ed.). Eugene, OR: Institute for the Development of Educational Achievement.

Good, R. H., III, Simmons, D. C., & Kame'enui, E. J. (2001). The importance and decision-making utility of a continuum of fluency-based indicators of foundational reading skills for third-grade high-stakes outcomes. *Scientific Studies of Reading, 5*(3), 257–288.

Goodman, K. S. (2006). *The truth about DIBELS: What it is, what it does.* Portsmouth, NH: Heinemann.

Hasbrouck, J. E., & Tindal, G. (1992). Curriculum-based oral reading fluency norms for students in grades 2 through 5. *Teaching Exceptional Children, 24*(3), 41–44.

Hintze, J. M., Shapiro, E. S., & Daly, E. J., III (1998). An investigation of the effects of passage difficulty level on outcomes of oral reading fluency progress monitoring. *School Psychology Review, 27*, 433–445.

Johnston, S. (2006). The fluency assessment system: Improving oral reading fluency with technology. In T. Rasinski, C. Blachowicz, & K. Lems (Eds.), *Fluency instruction: Research-based best practices* (pp. 123–140). New York: Guilford.

Leslie, L., & Caldwell, J. (2005). *Qualitative reading inventory–4* (4th ed.). Boston, MA: Allyn & Bacon.

Macmillan/McGraw-Hill. (1997). *Progress assessment: Reading, writing & listening.* New York: Author.

Marston, D. B. (1989). A curriculum-based measurement approach to assessing academic performance: What it is and why do it. In M. R. Shinn (Ed.), *Curriculum-based measurement: Assessing special children* (pp. 18–78). New York: Guilford.

Mathson, D. V., Allington, R. L., & Solic, K. L. (2006). Hijacking fluency and instructionally informative assessments. In T. Rasinski, C. Blachowicz, & K. Lems (Eds.), *Fluency instruction: Research-based best practices* (pp. 106–119). New York: Guilford Press.

Ohio Literacy Alliance. (2007). *Quick and easy high school reading assessments.* Retrieved December 10, 2007, from http://www.ohioliteracyalliance.org/fluency/fluency.htm

Rasinski, T. V. (1990b). Investigating measures of reading fluency. *Educational Research Quarterly, 14*(3), 37–44.

Rasinski, T. V. (2004a). *Assessing reading fluency.* Honolulu: Pacific Resources for Education and Learning. Retrieved December 10, 2007, from http://www.prel.org/products/re_/assessing-fluency.htm.

Rasinski, T. V. (2004c). *Multidimensional fluency scale*. Retrieved November 28, 2009, from www.ascd.org/publications/educational_leadership/mar04/vol61/num06/Creating_Fluent_Readers.aspx.

Rasinski, T. V., & Padak, N. (2005c). *3-minute reading assessments: Word recognition, fluency, and comprehension: Grades 1–4*. New York: Scholastic.

Rasinski, T. V., & Padak, N. (2005d). *3-minute reading assessments: Word recognition, fluency, and comprehension: Grades 5–8*. New York: Scholastic.

Samuels, S. J. (2007). The DIBELS tests: Is speed of barking at print what we mean by reading fluency? *Reading Research Quarterly, 42*, 563–566.

Scholastic. (1999). *Scholastic Reading Inventory using the Lexile Framework technical manual, forms A and B*. Retrieved May 25, 2009, from teacher.scholastic.com/products/sri/overview/lexiles.htm.

Wright Group. (1996). *SUNSHINE assessment guide: Grades K–1*. Bothell, WA: Author.

Comprehension and Fluency

Aslett, R. (1990). *Effects of the oral recitation lesson on reading comprehension of fourth grade developmental readers*. Unpublished doctoral dissertation, Brigham Young University, Provo, UT.

Comprehension Strategies Instruction. (2009). Huntington Beach, CA: Pacific Learning. Retrieved December 1, 2009, from www.pacificlearning.com.

Duke, N. K., Pressley, M., & Hilden, K. (2004). Difficulties with reading comprehension. In C. A. Stone, E. R. Silliman, B. J. Ehren, & K. Apel (Eds.), *Handbook of language and literacy: Development and disorders* (pp. 501–520). New York: Guilford.

Durkin, D. (1978). What classroom observations reveal about reading comprehension instruction. *Reading Research Quarterly, 14*, 481–533.

Fleischer, L. S., Jenkins, J. R., & Pany, D. (1979). Effects on poor readers' comprehension of training in rapid decoding. *Reading Research Quarterly, 15*, 30–48.

Fountas, I. C., & Pinnell, G. S. (2006). *Teaching for comprehending and fluency: Thinking, talking and writing about reading, K–8*. Portsmouth, NH: Heinemann.

Hamilton, C., & Shinn, M. R. (2000). Characteristics of word callers: An investigation of the accuracy of teachers' judgments of reading comprehension and oral reading skills. Eugene: University of Oregon. Retrieved June 1, 2009, from http://www.cbmnow.com/documents/wordcaller.pdf.

O'Shea, L. J., & Sindelar, P. T. (1983). The effects of segmenting written discourse on the reading comprehension of low- and high-performance readers. *Reading Research Quarterly, 18*, 458–465.

Rasinski, T. V., & Padak, N. D. (1998). How elementary students referred for compensatory reading instruction perform on school-based measures of word recognition, fluency, and comprehension. *Reading Psychology: An International Quarterly, 19*, 185–216.

Reutzel, D. R., & Hollingsworth, P. M. (1993). Effects of fluency training on second graders' reading comprehension. *Journal of Educational Research, 86*, 325–331.

Rose, M. (2004). *Week-by-week homework for building reading comprehension and fluency: Grades 3–6*. New York: Scholastic.

Willingham, D. (2006–2007). The usefulness of brief instruction in reading comprehension strategies. *American Educator, 30*(4), 39–50.

Prosody—Reading With Expression

Clay, M. M., & Imlach, R. H. (1971). Juncture, pitch, and stress as reading behavior variables. *Journal of Verbal Learning and Verbal Behavior, 10*, 133–139.

Dowhower, S. (1991). Speaking of prosody: Fluency's unattended bedfellow. *Theory into Practice, 30*(3), 165–175.

Schreiber, P. A. (1987). Prosody and structure in children's syntactic processing. In R. Horowitz & S. J. Samuels (Eds.), *Comprehending oral and written language* (pp. 243–270). New York: Academic Press.

Schreiber, P. A. (1991). Understanding prosody's role in reading acquisition. *Theory into Practice, 30*(3), 158–164.

Schreiber, P. A., & Read, C. (1980). Children's use of phonetic cues in spelling, parsing, and—maybe—reading. *Bulletin of the Orton Society, 30*, 209–224.

Prosody—Readers Theater

Carrick, L. U. (2000). *The effects of readers theatre on fluency and comprehension in fifth grade students in regular classrooms.* Unpublished doctoral dissertation, Lehigh University, Bethlehem, PA.

Carrick, L. U. (2006). Readers theatre across the curriculum. In T. Rasinski, C. Blachowicz, & K. Lems (Eds.), *Fluency instruction: Research-based best practices* (pp. 209–228). New York: Guilford.

Griffith, L., & Rasinski, T. V. (2002, November). *Readers theater promotes fluency and achievement.* Paper presented at the annual meeting of the College Reading Association, Philadelphia, PA.

Kozub, R. (2000, August). Reader's theater and its affect [*sic*] on oral language fluency. *Reading Online.* Retrieved November 28, 2009, from www.readingonline.org/editorial/august2000/rkrt.htm.

Martinez, M., Roser, N. L., & Strecker, S. (1999). "I never thought I could be a star": A readers theatre ticket to reading fluency. *The Reading Teacher, 52*, 326–334.

Millin, S. K., & Rinehart, S. D. (1999). Some of the benefits of readers theater participation for second-grade Title I readers. *Reading Research and Instruction, 39*(1), 71–88.

Prescott, J. O. (2003). The power of reader's theater. *Instructor, 112*(5), 22-26.

Rinehart, S. D. (1999). "Don't think for a minute that I'm getting up there": Opportunities for readers' theater in a tutorial for children with reading problems. *Reading Psychology: An International Quarterly, 20*, 71–89.

Tyler, B. J., & Chard, D. (2000). Using readers theater to foster fluency in struggling readers: A twist on the repeated reading strategy. *Reading and Writing Quarterly, 16*, 163–168.

Worthy, J. (2005). *Readers theater for building fluency: Strategies and scripts for making the most of this highly effective, motivating, and research-based approach to oral reading.* New York: Scholastic.

Worthy, J., & Prater, K. (2002). "I thought about it all night": Readers theatre for reading fluency and motivation. *The Reading Teacher, 56*, 294–297.

Prosody—Singing and Poetry-Based Approaches to Fluency

Biggs, M., Homan, S., Dedrick, R., & Rasinski, T. (2008). Using an interactive singing software program: A comparative study of middle school struggling readers. *Reading Psychology: An International Quarterly, 29*, 195–213.

Lems, K. (2001, fall). Integrated poetry performance unit. *ELI Teaching: A Journal of Theory and Practice, 34*, 44–45.

Lems, K. (2002). An American poetry project for low intermediate ESL adults. *English Teaching Forum.* Washington, DC: United States Information Agency. Available at: http://eca.state.gov/forum/vols/vol39/no4/p24.html]

Park, S. (2010, March). Fluency podcasts: Third grade poetry reading to build fluency. Retrieved Oct. 2, 2010 from http://fluencypodcasts.podbean.com/# <http://fluencypodcasts.podbean.com/>

Perfect, K. A. (1999). Rhyme and reason: Poetry for the heart and head. *The Reading Teacher, 52*, 728–737.

Rasinski, T. V., & Zimmerman, B. S. (2001). *Phonics poetry: Teaching word families.* New York: Allyn & Bacon.

Prosody—Fluency and English Language Learners

Baker, S. K., & Good, R. (1995). Curriculum-based measurement of English reading with bilingual Hispanic students: A validation study with second-grade students. *School Psychology Review, 24,* 561–578.

Blum, I. H., Koskinen, P. S., Tennant, N., Parker, E. M., Straub, M., & Curry, C. (1995). Using audiotaped books to extend classroom literacy instruction into the homes of second-language learners. *Journal of Reading Behavior, 27,* 535–563.

Chow, P., & Cummins, J. (2003). Valuing multilingual and multicultural approaches to learning. In S. R. Schecter & J. Cummins (Eds.), *Multilingual education in practice: Using diversity as a resource* (pp. 32–60). Portsmouth, NH: Heinemann.

Koskinen, P. S., Blum, I. H., Bisson, S. A., Phillips, S. M., Creamer, T. S., & Baker, T. K. (1999). Shared reading, books, and audiotapes: Supporting diverse students in school and at home. *The Reading Teacher, 52,* 430–444.

Koskinen, P. S., Blum, I. H., Bisson, S. A., Phillips, S. M., Creamer, T. S., & Baker, T. K. (2000). Book access, shared reading, and audio models: The effects of supporting the literacy learning of linguistically diverse students in home and school. *Journal of Educational Psychology, 92,* 23–36.

Lems, K. (2006). Reading fluency and comprehension in adult English language learners. In T. Rasinski, C. Blachowicz, & K. Lems (Eds.), *Fluency instruction: Research-based best practices* (pp. 231–252). New York: Guilford Press.

Lems, K., Miller, L. D., & Soro, T. M. (2010). *Teaching reading to English language learners: Insights from linguistics.* New York: Guilford.

McCauley, J. K., & McCauley, D. S. (1992). Using choral reading to promote language learning for ESL students. *The Reading Teacher, 45,* 526–533.

Taguchi, E. (1997). The effects of repeated readings on the development of lower identification skills of FL readers. *Reading in a Foreign Language, 11,* 97–119.

Taguchi, E., & Gorsuch, G. J. (2002). Transfer effects on repeated EFL reading on reading new passages: A preliminary investigation. *Reading in a Foreign Language, 14,* 43–45.

Automaticity—Reading Rate

Biemiller, A. (1977). Relationships between oral reading rates for letters, words, and simple text in the development of reading achievement. *Reading Research Quarterly, 13,* 223–253.

Breznitz, Z. (2007). *Asynchrony: Timing differences between processing modalities can cause reading difficulties.* Retrieved March 15, 2008, from http://www.childrenofthecode.org/interviews/breznitz.htm#RateofReading

Carver, R. P. (1990). *Reading rate: A review of research and theory.* San Diego: Academic Press.

LaBerge, D., & Samuels, S. A. (1974). Toward a theory of automatic information processing in reading. *Cognitive Psychology, 6,* 293–323.

Rasinski, T. V. (2000). Speed does matter in reading. *The Reading Teacher, 54,* 146–151.

Automaticity—Repeated Reading

Bromage, B. K., & Mayer, R. E. (1986). Quantitative and qualitative effects of repetition on learning from technical text. *Journal of Educational Psychology, 78,* 271–278.

Carver, R. P., & Hoffman, J. V. (1981). The effect of practice through repeated reading on gain in reading ability using a computer-based instructional system. *Reading Research Quarterly, 16,* 374–390.

Dowhower, S. L. (1987). Effects of repeated reading on second-grade transitional readers' fluency and comprehension. *Reading Research Quarterly, 22,* 389–407.

Dowhower, S. L. (1994). Repeated reading revisited: Research into practice. *Reading and Writing Quarterly, 10*, 343–358.

Herman, P. A. (1985). The effect of repeated readings on reading rate, speech pauses, and word recognition accuracy. *Reading Research Quarterly, 20*, 553–564.

Koskinen, P. S., & Blum, I. H. (1984). Repeated oral reading and acquisition of fluency. In J. A. Niles, & L. A. Harris (Eds.), *Changing perspectives on research in reading/language processing and instruction* (33rd Yearbook of the National Reading Conference, pp. 183–187). Rochester, NY: National Reading Conference.

Koskinen, P. S., & Blum, I. H. (1986). Paired repeated reading: A classroom strategy for developing fluent reading. *The Reading Teacher, 40*, 70–75.

Martinez, M., & Roser, N. (1985). Read it again: The value of repeated readings during storytime. *The Reading Teacher, 38*, 782–786.

Mayer, R. E. (1983). Can you repeat that? Qualitative effects of repetition and advance organizers on learning from science prose. *Journal of Educational Psychology, 75*, 40–49.

McGraw, L. K. (2000). Parent tutoring in repeated reading: Effects of procedural adherence on fluency, maintenance, and intervention acceptability. *Dissertation Abstracts International, 60*(7-A), 2372.

Meyer, M. S., & Felton, R. H. (1999). Repeated reading to enhance fluency: Old approaches and new directions. *Annals of Dyslexia, 49*, 283–306.

Neill, K. (1980). Turn kids on with repeated reading. *Teaching Exceptional Children, 12*, 63–64.

Paige, D. D. (2006). Increasing fluency in disabled middle school readers: Repeated reading utilizing above grade level reading passages. *Reading Horizons, 46*(3), 167–181.

Rasinski, T. V. (1990a). Effects of repeated reading and listening-while-reading on reading fluency. *Journal of Educational Research, 83*, 147–150.

Samuels, S. J. (1997). The method of repeated readings. *The Reading Teacher, 50*, 376–382. (Original work published 1979)

Semonick, M. A. (2001). The effects of paired repeated reading on second graders' oral reading and on-task behavior. *Dissertation Abstracts International, 62* (3-1A), 914.

Sindelar, P. T., Monda, L. E., & O'Shea, L. J. (1990). Effects of repeated readings on instructional- and mastery-level readers. *Journal of Educational Research, 83*, 220–226.

Turpie, J., & Paratore, J. (1995). Using repeated reading to promote reading success in a heterogeneously grouped first grade. In K. A. Hinchman, D. J. Leu, & C. K. Kinzer (Eds.), *Perspectives on literacy research and practice* (44th yearbook of the National Reading Conference, pp. 255–263). Chicago: National Reading Conference.

Automaticity—Dyad and Paired Reading

Eldredge, J. L., & Quinn, D. W. (1988). Increasing reading performance of low-achieving second graders with dyad reading groups. *Journal of Educational Research, 82*, 40–46.

Morgan, A., Wilcox, B. R., & Eldredge, J. L. (2000). Effect of difficulty levels on second-grade delayed readers using dyad reading. *Journal of Educational Research, 94*, 113–119.

Morgan, R., & Lyon, E. (1979). Paired reading: A preliminary report on a technique for parental tuition of reading-retarded children. *Journal of Child Psychology and Psychiatry, 20*, 151–60.

Rasinski, T. V., & Fredericks, A. D. (1991). The Akron paired reading project. *The Reading Teacher, 44*, 514–515.

Topping, K. (1987a). Paired reading: A powerful technique for parent use. *The Reading Teacher, 40*, 608–614.

Topping, K. (1987b). Peer tutored paired reading: Outcome data from ten projects. *Educational Psychology, 7*, 133–145.

Topping, K. (1989). Peer tutoring and paired reading: Combining two powerful techniques. *The Reading Teacher, 42*, 488–494.

Topping, K. (1995). *Paired reading, spelling and writing.* New York: Cassell.

Accuracy—Word Study and Phonics

Bear, D. R., Invernizzi, M., Templeton, S., & Johnston, F. (2007). *Words their way: Word study for phonics, vocabulary, and spelling instruction* (4th ed.). New York: Prentice Hall.

Beck, I. L. (2005). *Making sense of phonics: The hows and whys.* New York: Guilford.

Beck, I. L., McKeown, M. G., & Kucan, L. (2002). *Bringing words to life: Robust vocabulary instruction.* New York: Guilford.

Blachowicz, C. L., & Fisher, P. (2005). *Teaching vocabulary in all classrooms* (3rd ed.). New York: Prentice Hall.

Clay, M. M. (1968). A syntactic analysis of reading errors. *Journal of Verbal Learning and Verbal Behavior, 7*, 434–438.

Clay, M. M. (1969). Reading errors and self correction behavior. *British Journal of Educational Psychology, 39*, 47–56.

Cunningham, P. M. (2004). *Phonics they use* (4th ed.). New York: Allyn & Bacon.

Fry, E. (1998). The most common phonograms. *The Reading Teacher, 51*, 620–622.

Fry, E., & Kress, J. (2006). *The reading teacher's book of lists* (5th ed.). San Francisco: Jossey-Bass.

Gaskins, I. W., Ehri, L. C., Cress, C., O'Hara, C., & Donnelly, K. (1996-1997). Procedures for word learning: Making discoveries about words. *The Reading Teacher, 50*, 312–327.

Gunning, T. (1995). Word building: A strategic approach to the teaching of phonics. *The Reading Teacher, 48*, 484–488.

Mathes, P. G., Torgesen, J. K., & Allor, J. H. (2001). The effects of peer-assisted literacy strategies for first-grade readers with and without additional computer-assisted instruction in phonological awareness. *American Educational Research Journal, 38*, 371–410.

Stahl, S. A. (1992). Saying the "p" word: Nine guidelines for exemplary phonics instruction. *The Reading Teacher, 45*, 618–625.

Accuracy—Oral Reading Miscues

Flynt, E. S., & Cooter, R. B. (2004). *Flynt-Cooter reading inventory for the classroom* (5th ed.). Columbus, OH: Merrill.

Goodman, K. S. (1965). A linguistic study of cues and miscues in reading. *Elementary English, 42*, 639–643.

Goodman, K. S., & Burke, C. L. (1973). *Theoretically based studies of patterns of miscues in oral reading performance* (USOE Project No. 90375). Washington, DC: U.S. Department of Health, Education, and Welfare.

Goodman, Y. M., & Burke, C. L. (1972). *Reading miscue inventory.* New York: MacMillan.

Goodman, Y. M., & Marek, A. M. (Eds.). (1996). *Retrospective miscue analysis: Revaluing readers and reading.* Katona, NY: Richard C. Owen.

Hoffman, J. V., & Clements, R. (1984). Reading miscues and teacher verbal feedback. *Elementary School Journal, 84*, 423–439.

Hoffman, J. V., O'Neal, S., Kastler, L., Clements, R., Segel, K., & Nash, M. F. (1984). Guided oral reading and miscue focused verbal feedback in second-grade classrooms. *Reading Research Quarterly, 19*, 367–384.

Leu, D. J. (1982). Oral reading error analysis: A critical review of research and application. *Reading Research Quarterly, 17*, 420–437.

Moore, R. A., & Aspegren, C. M. (2001). Reflective conversations between two learners: Retrospective miscue analysis. *Journal of Adolescent & Adult Literacy, 44,* 492–503.

Various Approaches to Promote Fluency

Bauer, J. F., & Anderson, R. S. (2001, December/January). A constructivist stretch: Preservice teachers meet preteens in a technology-based literacy project. *Reading Online, 5*(5). Retrieved February 24, 2008, from www.readingonline.org/articles/art_index.asp?HREF=bauer/index.html.

Beach, S. A. (1993). Oral reading instruction: Retiring the bird in the round. *Reading Psychology: An International Quarterly, 14,* 333–338.

Clayton, K. (2000). Broadcast media: Enhancing literacy through video production. *Reading Online.* Retrieved November 28, 2009, from www.readingonline.org/newliteracies/lit_index.asp?HREF=action/clayton/index.html.

Dahl, P. R. (1970). An experimental program for teaching high speed word recognition and comprehension skills. In J. E. Button, T. Lovitt, & T. Rowland (Eds.), *Communications research in learning disabilities and mental retardation* (pp. 33–65). Baltimore, MD: University Park Press.

Eldredge, J. L. (1990). Increasing reading performance of poor readers in the third grade by using a group assisted strategy. *Journal of Educational Research, 84,* 69–77.

Eldredge, J. L., & Butterfield, D. D. (1986). Alternatives to traditional reading instruction. *The Reading Teacher, 40,* 32–37.

Eldredge, J. L., Reutzel, D. R., & Hollingsworth, P. M. (1996). Comparing the effectiveness of two oral reading practices: Round-robin reading and the Shared Book Experience. *Journal of Literacy Research, 28,* 201–225.

Fawcett, G., & Rasinski, T. (2008). Fluency strategies for struggling readers. In S. Lenski & J. Lewis (Eds.), *Reading success for struggling adolescent readers* (pp. 155–169). New York: Guilford Press.

Fowler, M. C., Lindemann, L. M., Thacker-Gwaltney, S., & Invernizzi, M. (2002). *A second year of one-on-one tutoring: An intervention for second graders with reading difficulties* (CIERA Rep. No. 3-019). Ann Arbor, MI: Center for the Improvement of Early Reading Achievement.

Greene, F. (1979). Radio reading. In C. Pennock (Ed.), *Reading comprehension at four linguistic levels* (pp. 104–107). Newark, DE: International Reading Association.

Heckelman, R. G. (1969). A neurological impress method of reading instruction. *Academic Therapy, 4,* 277–282.

Hoffman, J. V. (1987). Rethinking the role of oral reading in basal instruction. *Elementary School Journal, 87,* 367–373.

Hoffman, J. V., & Crone, S. (1985). The oral recitation lesson: A research-derived strategy for reading in basal texts. In J. A. Niles & R. V. Lalik (Eds.), *Issues in literacy: A research perspective* (34th Yearbook of the National Reading Conference, pp. 76–83). Rockfort, NY: National Reading Conference.

Hollingsworth, P. M. (1978). An experimental approach to the impress method of teaching reading. *The Reading Teacher, 31,* 624–626.

Hoskisson, K. (1975a). The many facets of assisted reading. *Elementary English, 52,* 312–315.

Hoskisson, K. (1975b). Successive approximation and beginning reading. *Elementary School Journal, 75,* 442–451.

Invernizzi, M., Juel, C., & Rosemary, C. A. (1997). A community volunteer tutorial that works. *The Reading Teacher, 50,* 304–311.

Invernizzi, M., Rosemary, C., Juel, C., & Richards, H. C. (1997). At-risk readers and community volunteers: A three-year perspective. *Scientific Studies of Reading, 1,* 277–300.

Jackson, J. B., Paratore, J. R., Chard, D. J., & Garnick, S. (1999). An early intervention supporting the literacy learning of children experiencing substantial difficulty. *Learning Disabilities: Research and Practice, 14*, 254–267.

Knapp, N. F., & Winsor, A. P. (1998). A reading apprenticeship for delayed primary readers. *Reading Research and Instruction, 38*, 13–29.

McNaughton, S., Glynn, T., & Robinson, V. (1985). *Pause, prompt and praise: Effective tutoring for remedial reading.* Birmingham, United Kingdom: Positive Products.

Mercer, C. D., Campbell, K. U., Miller, M. D., Mercer, K. D., & Lane, H. B. (2000). Effects of a reading fluency intervention for middle schoolers with specific learning disabilities. *Learning Disabilities: Research and Practice, 15*, 179–189.

Morris, D., & Nelson, L. (1992). Supported oral reading with low achieving second graders. *Reading Research and Instruction, 32*(1), 49–63.

Morris, D., Shaw, B., & Perney, J. (1990). Helping low readers in grades 2 and 3: An after-school volunteer tutoring program. *Elementary School Journal, 91*, 133–150.

Moskal, M. K., & Blachowicz, C. (2006). *Partnering for fluency* (Tools for teaching literacy). New York: Guilford.

Myers, C. A. (1978). Reviewing the literature on Fernald's technique of remedial reading. *The Reading Teacher, 31*, 614–619.

Opitz, M. F., & Rasinski, T. V. (1998). *Good-bye round robin: 25 effective oral reading strategies.* Portsmouth, NH: Heinemann.

Reitsma, P. (1988). Reading practice for beginners: Effects of guided reading, reading-while-listening, and independent reading with computer-based speech. *Reading Research Quarterly, 23*, 219–235.

Searfoss, L. (1975). Radio Reading. *The Reading Teacher, 29*, 295–296.

Stallings, J. (1980). Allocated academic learning time revisited, or beyond time on task. *Educational Researcher, 9*, 11–16.

Sweeney, A. (2004a). *Fluency lessons for the overhead: Grades 2–3.* New York: Scholastic.

Sweeney, A. (2004b). *Fluency lessons for the overhead: Grades 4–6.* New York: Scholastic.

Specific Programs to Promote Fluency

Carbo, M. (1978a). Teaching reading with talking books. *The Reading Teacher, 32*, 267–273.

Carbo, M. (1978b). A word imprinting technique for children with severe memory disorders. *Teaching Exceptional Children, 11*(1), 3–5.

Carbo, M. (1981). Making books talk to children. *The Reading Teacher, 35*, 186–189.

Carbo, M. (1989). *How to record books for maximum reading gains.* Long Island, NY: National Reading Styles Institute.

Clay, M. M. (1993). *Reading Recovery: A guidebook for teachers in training.* Portsmouth, NH: Heinemann.

D'Agostino, J. V., & Murphy, J. A. (2004). A meta-analysis of Reading Recovery in United States schools. *Educational Evaluation and Policy Analysis, 26*(1), 23–38.

Florida Center for Reading Research. (2006). *Fluency First!* [Review]. Retrieved September 5, 2006, from http://www.fcrr.org/FCRRReports/PDF/FluencyFirstR2.pdf.

Fluency Instruction. (2007). Reading Recovery Council of North America. Retrieved October 26, 2009, from http://www.readingrecovery.org/reading_recovery/federal/Essential/fluency.asp.

Hasbrouck, J. E., Ihnot, C., & Rogers, G. H. (1999). "Read Naturally": A strategy to increase oral reading fluency. *Reading Research and Instruction, 39*(1), 27–38.

Hecker, L., Burns, L, Elkind, J., Elkind, K., & Katz, L. (2002). Benefits of assistive reading software for students with attention disorders. *Annals of Dyslexia, 52,* 243–272.

Langford, J. (2001, July). Tape assisted reading for a group of low progress readers in a secondary school. *Reading Today for Tomorrow, Auckland [NZ] Reading Association Newsletter,* 14–21.

Morris, D. (1995). *Early Steps: An early intervention program.* Bloomington, IN: ERIC Clearinghouse on Reading, English, and Communication. (ERIC Document Reproduction Service No. ED388956).

Morris, D., Tyner, B., & Perney, J. (2000). Early Steps: Replicating the effects of a first-grade reading intervention program. *Journal of Educational Psychology, 92,* 681–693.

Nalder, S. (2002). *The effectiveness of Rainbow Reading: An audio-assisted reading program.* Huntington Beach, CA: Pacific Learning. Retrieved November 27, 2009, from www.rainbowreading.co.nz/whatis.htm#research.

Padak, N., & Rasinski, T. (2005). *Fast Start for early readers: A research-based, send-home literacy program with 60 reproducible poems and activities that ensures reading success for every child.* New York: Scholastic.

Pearson, P. D. (2004). *The influence of Reading Recovery on everyday classroom practice. Reading Recovery New Zealand.* Retrieved October 26, 2009, from www.readingrecovery.ac.nz/institute/downloads/davidpearson_slideshow.ppt.

Pluck, M. (1995a). *Rainbow Reading programme: Teachers' manual.* Nelson, New Zealand: Rainbow Reading Programme Ltd.

Pluck, M. (1995b). Rainbow Reading programme: Using taped stories. *Reading Forum, 1,* 25–30.

Pluck, M. (1995c). *Rainbow Reading programme: Using taped stories—The Nelson Project.* Auckland: New Zealand Reading Association.

Pluck, M. (2006). "Jonathan is 11 but reading like a struggling 7-year-old": Providing assistance for struggling readers with a tape-assisted reading program. In T. V. Rasinski, C. Blachowicz, & K. Lems (Eds.), *Fluency instruction: Research-based best practices* (pp.192–208). New York: Guilford.

Rainbow Reading programme. (2009). Retrieved December 1, 2009, from www.rainbowreading.co.nz.

Rasinski, T. V. (1995). Fast Start: A parental involvement reading program for primary grade students. In W. Linek & E. Sturtevant (Eds.), *Generations of literacy* (17th Yearbook of the College Reading Association, pp. 301–312). Harrisonburg, VA: College Reading Association.

Rasinski, T. V., & Padak, N. D. (2005b). *Fluency First! Daily routines to develop reading fluency.* Columbus, OH: Wright Group/McGraw-Hill.

Rasinski, T., & Stevenson, B. (2005). The effects of Fast Start reading, a fluency-based home involvement reading program, on the reading achievement of beginning readers. *Reading Psychology: An International Quarterly, 26,* 109–125.

Renaissance Learning. (2006). *STAR Reading.* Wisconsin Rapids, WI: Author. Retrieved Nov. 29, 2009, from www.renlearn.com/starreading/overview/default.htm.

Santa, C. M., & Hoien, T. (1999). An assessment of Early Steps: A program for early intervention of reading problems. *Reading Research Quarterly, 34,* 54–79.

Stevenson, B. (2002). *Efficacy of the Fast Start parent tutoring program in the development of reading skills of first grade students.* Unpublished doctoral dissertation, Ohio State University, Columbus.

Wheldall, K. (2000). Does Rainbow Repeated Reading add value to an intensive literacy intervention program for low-progress readers? An experimental evaluation. *Educational Review, 52*(1), 29–36.

General Resources on Reading Instruction

Allington, R. L. (2000). What really matters for struggling readers. New York: Allyn & Bacon.

Allington, R. L., & McGill-Franzen, A. (2003). The impact of summer setback on the reading achievement gap. *Phi Delta Kappan, 84,* 68–75.

Anderson, R. C., Wilson, P. T., & Fielding, L. G. (1988). Growth in reading and how children spend their time outside of school. *Reading Research Quarterly, 23*, 285–303.

Blair, T. R., Rupley, W. H., & Nichols, W. D. (2007). The effective teacher of reading: Considering the "what" and "how" of instruction. *The Reading Teacher, 60*, 432–438.

Chall, J. S. (1996). *Stages of reading development* (2nd ed.). Fort Worth, TX: Harcourt-Brace.

Chomsky, C. (1976). After decoding: What? *Language Arts, 53*, 288–296.

Clay, M. M. (2005a). *Literacy lessons designed for individuals, Part One: Why? When? And How?* Portsmouth, NH: Heinemann.

Clay, M. M. (2005b). Literacy lessons designed for individuals, Part Two: Teaching procedures. Portsmouth, NH: Heinemann.

Coles, G. (2004). Danger in the classroom: "Brain glitch" research and learning to read. *Phi Delta Kappan, 85*, 344–351.

Daniels, H. (1994). *Literature circles: Voice and choice in the student-centered classroom.* York, ME: Stenhouse.

Ehri, L. C. (2005). Learning to read words: Theory, findings, and issues. *Scientific Studies of Reading, 9*, 167–188.

Fountas, I. C., & Pinnell, G. S. (1996). *Guided reading: Good first teaching for all children.* Portsmouth, NH: Heinemann.

Fountas, I. C., & Pinnell, G. S. (2001). *Guiding readers and writers: Teaching comprehension, genre, and content literacy.* Portsmouth, NH: Heinemann.

Gallagher, K. (2004). *Deeper reading: Comprehending challenging texts 4–12.* Portland, ME: Stenhouse.

Harris, T. L., & Hodges, R. E. (Eds.). (1995). *The literacy dictionary: The vocabulary of reading and writing.* Newark, DE: International Reading Association.

Henkin, R., Dipinto, V., & Hunt, J. (Eds.). (2002). Critical literacy in democratic classrooms [Themed issue]. *Democracy and Education, 14*(3).

Hoffman, J. V. (1991). Teacher and school effects in learning to read. In R. Barr, M. L. Kamil, P. Mosenthal, & P. D. Pearson (Eds.), *Handbook of reading research: Vol. 2* (pp. 911–950). White Plains, NY: Longman.

Hoffman, J. V., Roser, N. L., Salas, R., Patterson, E., & Pennington, J. (2001). Text leveling and "little books" in first-grade reading. *Journal of Literacy Research, 33*(3), 507–528.

Liben, D., & Liben, M. (2004). Our journey to reading success. *Educational Leadership, 61*(6), 58–61.

Liben, D., & Liben, M. (2005). Learning to read in order to learn: Building a program for upper elementary students. *Phi Delta Kappan, 86*, 401–406.

McGee, L. M., & Mandel-Morrow, L. (2005). *Teaching literacy in kindergarten.* New York: Guilford.

McGill-Franzen, A., & Allington, R. L. (2005). *Bridging the summer reading gap.* Retrieved October 28, 2009, from teacher.scholastic.com/products/instructor/summer_reading.htm.

Mraz, M., & Rasinski, T. V. (2007). Summer reading loss. *The Reading Teacher, 60*, 784–789.

National Institute of Child Health and Human Development (NICHD). (2000a). *Report of the National Reading Panel. Teaching children to read: An evidence-based assessment of the scientific research literature on reading and its implications for reading instruction* (NIH Publication No. 00-4769). Washington, DC: U.S. Government Printing Office.

National Institute of Child Health and Human Development (NICHD). (2000b). *Report of the National Reading Panel. Teaching children to read: Report of the subgroups* (NIH Publication No. 00-4754). Washington, DC: U.S. Government Printing Office.

Postlethwaite, T. N., & Ross, K. N. (1992). *Effective schools in reading: Implications for policy planners.* The Hague: International Association for the Evaluation of Educational Achievement.

Rasinski, T. V., & Padak, N. (2004). *Effective reading strategies: Teaching children who find reading difficult* (3rd ed.). Columbus, OH: Merrill/Prentice Hall.

Rosenblatt, L. (1978). *The reader, the text, and the poem: The transactional theory of literary work.* Carbondale: Southern Illinois University Press.

Smith, F. (2006). *Reading without nonsense* (4th ed.). New York: Teachers College Press.

Smith, J., & Elley, W. (1997). *How children learn to read: Insights from the New Zealand experience.* Katonah, NY: Richard C. Owen.

Snow, C. E., Burns, M. S., & Griffin, P. (Eds.). (1998). *Preventing reading difficulties in young children.* Washington, DC: National Academies Press.

Tompkins, G. E. (2006). *Literacy for the 21st century: A balanced approach* (4th ed.). Columbus, OH: Merrill Prentice Hall.

Trabasso, T., & Suh, S. (1993). Understanding text: Achieving explanatory coherence through online inferences and mental operations in working memory. *Discourse Processes, 16*(1/2), 3–34.

Vacca, J. L., Vacca, R. T., & Gove, M. K. (2000). *Reading and learning to read.* New York: Allyn & Bacon.

Walker, B. J. (2003). The cultivation of student self-efficacy in reading and writing. *Reading and Writing Quarterly, 19*, 173–187.

Wilkinson, I., Wardrop, J. L., & Anderson, R. C. (1988). Silent reading reconsidered: Reinterpreting reading instruction and its effects. *American Educational Research Journal, 25*, 127–144.

Zeigler, L. L., & Johns, J. L. (2005). *Visualization: Using mental images to strengthen comprehension.* Dubuque, IA: Kendall/Hunt.

References for Other Works Mentioned

Berliner, D., & Casanova, U. (1997). *Putting research to work in your school.* New York: Scholastic.

Blymire, L. A., Brunner, T. L., Jones, C. J., & Knauer, D. B. (1982). *A.C.T. 1: Affective cognitive thinking: Thinking strategies for the gifted.* Hightstown, NJ: Penns Valley Publishers.

Board of Studies, New South Wales. (2000). How we learn what we need to know: A selection of literacy and numeracy case studies that have enhanced outcomes for Aboriginal students. Retrieved Jan. 18, 2007, from http://www.boardofstudies.nsw.edu.au/aboriginal_research/pdf_doc/aborlitnum_howwelearn.pdf.

Bunting, E. (1999). *Smoky night.* New York: HarperCollins.

Coerr, E. (2005). *Sadako and the thousand paper cranes.* London: Puffin.

Cowley, J. (1990). The farm concert. DeSoto, TX: Wright Group.

Cowley, J. (1996). Yuck soup. DeSoto, TX: Wright Group.

Cowley, J. (1998). The birthday cake. DeSoto, TX: Wright Group.

Cronin, D. (2000). Click, clack, moo: Cows that type. New York: Simon & Schuster.

Epstein, J. (1984). School policy and parent involvement: Research results. *Educational Horizons, 62*, 70–72.

Fisher, C. W., & Berliner, D. C. (Eds.). (1985). *Perspectives on instructional time.* New York: Longman.

Florian, D. (2002). *Insectlopedia.* New York: Harcourt.

Florian, D. (2002). "The Daddy Longlegs." In *Insectlopedia.* New York: Harcourt.

Florian, D. (2005). *Omnibeasts.* New York: Harcourt.

Gass, S., & Selinker, L. (2000). *Second language acquisition: An introductory course* (2nd ed.). Mahwah, NJ: Lawrence Erlbaum.

Hayward, L., & Goldsmith, C. (1995). *I am not going to read any words today! Learn about rhyming words.* [Adapted from original by Dr. Seuss.] New York: Scholastic.

Henderson, A. (1988). Parents are a school's best friend. *Phi Delta Kappan, 70,* 148–153.

Houghton Mifflin Reading: The nation's choice. (2003). Boston, MA: Houghton Mifflin.

National Parent Teacher Association. (1997). PTA issues: Standards for parent involvement in education. *Reading Today, 14,* 16–25.

Parkinson, K. (1986). The enormous turnip. Morton Grove, IL: Albert Whitman.

Polacco, P. (1992). Chicken Sunday. New York: Philomel Books.

Prelutsky, J. (1984). *The new kid on the block.* New York: Greenwillow Books.

Prelutsky, J. (2002). *Scranimals.* New York: HarperCollins.

Prelutsky, J. (2006). *Behold the bold umbrellaphant and other poems.* New York: HarperCollins.

Progress assessment: Reading, writing, & listening. (1997). New York: Macmillan/McGraw-Hill.

Promoting teachers as researchers. (2004). *Reading Today,* 22(2), 7.

Pugliano-Martin, C. (1999). 25 just-right plays for emergent readers. New York: Scholastic.

Rylant, C. (1996). *An angel for Solomon Singer.* New York: Scholastic.

Safari Magazine. Mondo Publishing.

Sendak, M. (1964). Where the wild things are. New York: HarperCollins.

Seuss, Dr. (1957). *The cat in the hat.* New York: Random House.

Sierra-Perry, M. (1996). *Standards in practice: Grades 3–5.* Urbana, IL: National Council of Teachers of English.

Silverstein, S. (1993). *A giraffe and a half.* New York: HarperCollins.

Silverstein, S. (2002). *Who wants a cheap rhinoceros?* New York: Simon and Schuster Children's Publishing.

Williams, D. L., & Chavkin, N. F. (1989). Essential elements of strong parent involvement programs. *Educational Leadership, 47*(2), 18–20.